Prayer for beginners
and those
who have forgotten how

Mark Link, S.J.

Argus Communications
A Division of DLM, Inc.
Allen, Texas 75002 U.S.A.

Photo Credits

Isac Jo, cover
Algimantas Kezys, S.J., book

Acknowledgements

All biblical quotes are from *Today's English Version* of the Bible, © American Bible Society, 1966, 1971, 1976. All rights reserved.

From *Room for Me and a Mountain Lion: Poetry of Open Space.* Selected by Nancy Larrick. Copyright © 1974 by Nancy Larrick. Reprinted by permission of publisher, M. Evans & Company, Inc., New York.

From *Hungry for God,* © 1974 by Ralph Martin. By permission of Doubleday & Co., Inc.

Excerpt from "The Magic of Good Posture," by Warren R. Young, *The Reader's Digest* November 1971. Copyright © 1971 by The Reader's Digest Assn., Inc.

Excerpt from "Oriental Mysticism and Christian Prayer," by William Johnston, S.J. *Review for Religious* March 1970. By permission.

Based on "How to Pray," by Bernard Basset, S.J., which was prepared for the Sacred Heart Program Television and reprinted in the July, August, and September 1970 issues of the *Canadian Messenger of the Sacred Heart.*

From *The One and Only Me,* By Irene Champernowne. © 1975 by Argus Communications and © 1974, Irene Champernowne. Also published by the National Christian Education Council.

From "Benedict Arnold Seagull," by Philip Yancey, *Campus Life,* © 1975. Reprinted by permission of Campus Life Magazine, Youth for Christ International, Wheaton, Ill.

From "Morality According to Snoopy," by Don Brophy, *Ave Maria* April 1969. By permission.

Excerpt from "You," May 2, 1974. © The Thomas More Assn.

From *The Power and the Glory,* by Graham Greene. © 1960 by Graham Greene. Reprinted by permission of Viking Press.

Reprinted by permission of William Morrow & Company, Inc., from *Zen and the Art of Motorcycle Maintenance,* by Robert M. Pirsig. Copyright © 1974 by Robert M. Pirsig. Also by permission of the Bodley Head Ltd.

Excerpt from "The Special Joys of Super-Slow Reading," by Sidney Piddington. Reprinted with permission from the June 1973 *Reader's Digest.* Copyright 1973 by the Reader's Digest Assn., Inc.

From *A Terrible Beauty* by James Carroll. © 1973 by the Missionary Society of St. Paul the Apostle in the State of N. Y. Published by Newman Press. By permission.

Excerpt from "The Man Who Was Afraid of Water," by Lois Briener, © 1975 *Campus Life.* Reprinted by permission from Campus Life Magazine, Youth for Christ International, Wheaton, Ill.

ARGUS COMMUNICATIONS
A Division of DLM, Inc.
One DLM Park,
Allen, Texas 75002 U.S.A.

International Standard Book Number:
0-913592-78-1

Library of Congress Number: 76-41584

20 19 18 17 16 15 14 13 12 11

From "Apollo 15: Three Views of the Moon," by Col. James B. Irwin. Copyright © 1971 by *The New York Times* Company. Reprinted in Readers Digest Nov. 1971. Reprinted by permission.

From *In God's Underground,* by Richard Wurmbrand. © Diane Publishing Co., 1968.

From "Malcolm X Is Alive," by Raymond A. Schroth, *America,* April 22, 1967. Reprinted by permission.

From *The Autobiography of Malcolm X,* by Malcolm X, asst. Haley. © 1966 by Grove Press. Reprinted by permission of Grove Press and Hutchinson Publishing Group Ltd.

From "Religious Life: Contemplative Life," by William Johnston, S.J. *Review for Religious* March 1969. Reprinted by permission.

From "Meditation: The Newest and Oldest Quest," by Joseph Grassi. Reprinted by permission of *St. Anthony Messenger.*

From "Beyond Politics, the Reality of Faith," adapted from "The Presidency," a *LIFE* feature by Hugh Sidey. © Time Inc.

From *Dawn Without Darkness,* by Anthony T. Padovano. © 1971 by the Missionary Society of St. Paul the Apostle in the State of New York. Used by permission of Pastoral Educational Services.

From *Belief in Human Life,* by Anthony T. Padovano. © 1969 by the Missionary Society of St. Paul the Apostle in the State of N. Y. Permission by Pastoral Educational Services.

From *The Allelulia Affair,* by Malcolm Boyd. © 1975. Used by permission of Word Books, Waco, Texas.

Adapted from "Builder of Bridges for Us Poor Devils," by Morris West, *LIFE* Magazine, © Time, Inc. Reprinted by permission.

From *Journal of a Soul,* by Pope John XXIII. © 1965 Geoffrey Chapman Ltd. Used with permission of McGraw-Hill Book Co.

Reprinted with permission of Farrar, Straus & Giroux, Inc. from *Thoughts in Solitude,* by Thomas Merton. © 1956, 1958 by the Abbey of Our Lady of Gethsemane. Also by permission of Curtis Brown, Ltd.

From *The Secret of Staying in Love,* by John Powell. © 1974 by Argus Communications.

From *Nobel,* by Nicholas Halasz. © 1959 by Nicholas Halasz by permission of Grossman Publishers.

From "Teach Us to Pray," by Stephen Doyle. With permission of HI-TIME, the weekly religion text for high school, Milwaukee.

From *Prayers: For Daily and Occasional Use,* by Rev. Victor Hoagland, C.P. © 1969 Passionist Missions. Published by Paulist Press.

From "Progress in Prayer," by Michael Lapierre, Copyright © 1970, *The Way.*

From *Our Prayer* by Louis Evely © 1970 by Herder and Herder, Inc. Used by permission of The Seabury Press.

From *WORKING: People Talk About What They Do All Day and How They Feel About What They Do,* by Studs Terkel. © 1972, 1974 by Studs Terkel. Reprinted by permission of Pantheon Books, a division of Random House, Inc. and Wildwood House Limited.

From *Four Screenplays of Ingmar Bergman.* © 1960 by Ingmar Bergman. Reprinted by permission of Simon & Schuster, Inc.

Adapted from *Alive: The Story of the Andes Survivors,* by Piers Paul Read. © 1974 by Piers Paul Read. Reprinted by permission of J.B. Lippincott Co.

From "What Man Can Be," by Bob Richards. © 1968 Guideposts Associates, Inc., Carmel, N.Y. Used by permission of *GUIDEPOSTS MAGAZINE.*

From *The Farther Reaches of Human Nature,* by Abraham Maslow. © 1971 by Bertha G. Maslow. By permission of Viking Press.

Excerpt from "Hurray! It's Raining!" by Elizabeth Starr Hill, *Reader's Digest* April 1967. © 1967 by the Reader's Digest Assn., Inc.

Contents

How this book came about

Three years ago
I began to teach young people, in a school setting,
how to pray.

The program grew like the mustard seed
in the Gospel.
Soon other teachers, both lay and religious,
became involved.
Details of our program will be found in the Appendix.

Now we would like to share our how-to-pray program
with others.
We hope it will help:

individuals
as a do-it-yourself guide
for learning to pray,

groups
as a program for learning and
sharing prayer together,

teachers
as a method of teaching prayer
to young people.

Groups may wish to begin with Chapter 7.
The exercises following the chapter are ideal
for introducing a group, gradually, to shared prayer.

Mark Link, S.J.

1

You: the person

Backpacking

A horseback trip has its special glory,
but to move into harmony with the wilderness,
there is nothing like backpacking.
Steadily you push on,
carrying everything you need to survive,
and at the same time
seeing details of rocks and plants and wildlife
no horseback rider can possibly take in. . . .

Whether such experiences make a poet
or whether the poet seeks them out
I do not know.
But the fact is that many poets—
particularly our modern poets—
have turned from the brutal turmoil of urban living
to explore rocky trails
or follow animal tracks across the snow.

Nancy Larrick
Room for Me and a Mountain Lion

Prayer places

There is something about the outdoors
that attracts not only poets but also pray-ers.
One of the greatest teachers of pray-ers
seems to have preferred the outdoors for his own
personal meditation. We read in the Gospels:

Jesus went up a hill to pray.
Luke 6:12

Jesus went to a lonely place, where he prayed.
Mark 1:35

But Jesus also recommended praying indoors
in complete privacy:

Go to your room and close the door,
and pray to your Father who is unseen.
Matthew 6:6

Origen told second-century Christians:

Any place can be suitable for prayer. . . .
But if we want to pray without being disturbed,
we would do well, if possible,
to find a special place in our own home,
a consecrated place, so to speak—and pray there.

A private place for prayer has several advantages.
For example,
you might wish to pray lying down.
Or, during prayer, you might feel moved
to lift your arms to the sky.
Or you might want to sigh, cry, or speak out loud.
In a public place, you would hesitate to do this.
Your prayer would lack freedom and spontaneity.

Some places that modern Christians have found
suitable for private prayer are:

- the back of a church or chapel,

- your own bedroom,

- a little-used room in your home,

- a secluded spot outdoors.

The important thing about a prayer place
is that it helps us to pray better.
Picking the right place
is one of the keys to effective prayer.

Prayer times

In *Hungry for God,* Ralph Martin writes:

*A real estate man I know
gets up early in the morning to pray;
an aerospace engineer
prays and reads Scripture on his lunch hour;
a production manager of a computing firm
prays after the children are in bed at night.*

Reporting on *times* Jesus chose for prayer,
the Gospels say:

*Very early the next morning,
Jesus went to a lonely place, where he prayed.*
Mark 1:35

*Jesus went up a hill to pray,
and spent the whole night there praying to God.*
Luke 6:12

Martin goes on to note that
the demands of modern living are such
that if we don't have a schedule for prayer,
we probably won't pray.
Some people don't like scheduling prayer.
They say: "It's not spontaneous."

If you think for a moment, however,
when other activities become important to us,
we don't leave them to chance.
They pass from the spontaneous and haphazard
to the scheduled and committed.
Martin gives this example:

If two people want to become more than mere
acquaintances, they need to agree on definite times
and places to get together. . . .
Romantic ideas about spontaneity are just that:
romantic and not realistic.

But there is still room for spontaneity.
Prayer will often surprise us by coming unexpectedly,
just as a friend surprises us
by showing up unexpectedly.

Unless there is a commitment to fixed times,
however, there is not likely to be much prayer.
That's just the way we human beings are made.

Four popular times for prayer
that people have tried and found helpful are:

- after rising and showering in the morning,

- during the noon lunch break,

- after returning from work, before supper,

- immediately before retiring.

Finding the right schedule for daily prayer
is going to take experimentation and dedication.
Getting a schedule that fits your life-style
may take months, but it is worth the effort.
Prayer is that important.

Prayer posture

Warren Young begins a captivating article:

*How much would you give
for a formula that guaranteed to make you look
younger, brighter, more attractive—
and feel that way too? Probably a lot.
Yet the secret is built right into the human body,
your body.
All you have to do is take a few minutes
every now and then to check up on your posture.*

"The Magic of Good Posture"

The author then goes on to discuss
the amazing effect
that our posture has on the way we feel and think.

Posture also plays a key role in the way we pray.
William Johnston writes in "Oriental Mysticism
and Christian Prayer":

*If you go to a Zen temple. . . .
you are immediately taught
how to gather yourself together in concentration. . . .*

*The first thing is control of the body. . . .
Eastern religions know how to put the body
at the service of prayer. . . .
In the Bhagavad Gita we find instructions
that are remarkably similar to Zen.*

*The Yogin is told to select a clean place,
neither too high nor yet too low,
and there he sits in magnificent silence,
his mind at rest—*

"as a lamp might stand in a windless place,
unflickering."
He is to restrain all his thoughts and senses;
his mind is reduced to a single point;

"Remaining still,
let him keep body, head and neck
In a straight line, unmoving;
Let him fix his gaze. . . .
Not looking round about him."

"There let him sit,
his self all stilled
His fear all gone. . .
His mind controlled, his thoughts on Me,
Integrated, yet intent on Me."

Just as you can pray anywhere and anytime,
so you can pray in any posture.
A popular position in Western culture
has been kneeling.
It has its origin in the Bible itself:

Just before Stephen was killed by a mob,

he fell to his knees and cried out in a loud voice,
"Lord! Do not remember this sin against them!"

Acts 7:60

When friends saw Paul and Luke off on ship,
Luke writes:

We all knelt down on the beach and prayed.

Acts 21:5

Although kneeling was a popular prayer posture
in biblical times,
it was by no means the only one.
Moses prayed before the burning bush face down.
Jesus probably prayed in this same position
during his agony in the garden.

Commenting on lying face down or on your back,
one spiritual writer notes:

When you think of it,
the majority of people die lying down.
Beyond the vividness of this act of humility
lies the value of relaxation in prayer.

Origen wrote:

Of the many postures the body can assume
the most preferable
is extending the hands and raising the eyes.
For the body is then showing the soul
how it should behave in prayer. . . .
But circumstances may arise
in which it is better for us to pray sitting. . .
even lying down.

In the final analysis,
the best posture is the one that helps you to pray.
Here are some recommended positions:

- Lie on your bed or the floor, legs flat,
  heels together, and eyes fixed on the ceiling.

- Sit erect in a chair, both feet on the floor,
  hands in your lap or resting palms down
  on the arms of the chair.

- Kneel upright at your bed, back straight,
  hands resting on the bed for support.

- Sit on the floor, legs crossed and pulled
  in toward the body, back straight and
  pressed against the wall, hands in lap
  or on knees with palms open up or down.

This latter posture deserves special attention.
Unlike a posture of sitting or lying down,
the cross-legged posture
carries with it no associations of study or rest.
It breaks with all associations
and speaks only of a special occupation: prayer.

Moreover, the cross-legged, straight-back posture
carries with it a paradox of repose and alertness.
Those who adopt this posture
say that they come from prayer consistently refreshed—
physically as well as spiritually.
The posture may take a week or 2 to get used to,
but the time and effort are immensely worth it.

Prayer mood

After choosing a place, time, and posture,
the next step is to create a mental climate for prayer.
Some methods that people have found helpful
are the following.

Breathing

Take the position you intend to use in prayer.
Next, relax your body.
Begin with the muscles of your face and move down
through your shoulders, chest, arms, and legs.

Now, observe your breathing. Don't change it,
just observe it.

> Is your breathing smooth?
> If it is jerky, slowly even it out.
>
> Is your breathing deep?
> If it is shallow, gently deepen it.
>
> Is your breathing rapid?
> If so, gradually, slow it down.

Close your eyes and try to establish a pattern
of slow, deep, even breathing.
Continue this until a mood of concentration sets in.

Listening

Take your prayer position and relax your body.
Close your eyes and listen to the sounds around you.
Let them penetrate your being—freely and deeply.
Continue this until a mood of quiet sets in.

Alternate listening: Close your ears with your
thumbs, close your eyes, and listen to your own
breathing.
After 8 breaths, return your hands to their normal
prayer position. Keeping your eyes closed,
listen to the sounds around you:
the softest, the farthest.

Sounds distract us only when we try to fight them.
Allow the sounds to penetrate your being—
freely and deeply—until a mood of quiet begins.

Heartbeat

Take your prayer position and relax your body.
Close your eyes and listen to your heartbeat.
When you become aware of it, monitor its rhythm.
Monitor it until a mood of interior focus begins.

Sensation

Take your prayer position and relax your body.
Become aware of your clothes gripping your
shoulders, legs, arms; your shoes gripping your
feet; the chair gripping your body.
Monitor these sensations until relaxation sets in.

As with other aspects of the prayer process,
creating the "mood" for prayer
will vary from person to person.
Trial and error is the only way to discover
what works best for you.

Presence of God

After the place, time, posture, and mood
have been taken care of,
you are ready for the key step in the prayer process:
opening yourself to God's presence.
Bernard Basset writes:

I must
stop thinking of everything else for the moment,
while I stand and put myself in the presence of God,
becoming aware that He is in the room with me.

This awareness of God's presence
is a great gift.
If God gives it to me, as He does from time to time,
then I do no more
than stand or sit or kneel in His presence.

Any effort on my part
to make myself feel that God is there
is nearly always wrong.
I cannot move an inch in prayer unless the Lord leads me.

Sometimes an object outside myself
(crucifix, statue, picture)
which I associate with prayer
will help me to meet God.
"How to Pray"

Sometimes, closing your eyes,
fixing them on a blank wall, or focusing them
midway between yourself and a wall
best serves the purpose of prayer.

Armand Nigro also stresses
the importance of the opening minutes of prayer:

*Peacefully
remind yourself how present God is to you. . . .
This takes a little time,
but it should always be done and never rushed.
You should not hurry that part of your prayer,
even if it takes the whole time. . . .*

*In these moments
God's special communication may come
with that deep personal sense of His presence.
Sometimes
He makes His presence felt (experienced) by us.
And when He does, let it continue;
Let this experience hold or carry you,
just as water holds up a floating body.
Stay with it until it fades.*

"Prayer—A Personal Response to God's Presence"

Here are some prayers, asking God to help you
to open yourself to his presence.
Each fits with one of the 4 mood-building exercises:

breathing,
listening,
heartbeat,
sensation.

After each exercise,
pray slowly and reflectively the appropriate prayer:

- "Father,
  you are closer to me
  than my own breath.
  May each breath I take
  deepen my awareness of your presence."

- "Father,
  you are as real
  as the sounds around me.
  May each sound I hear
  deepen my awareness of your reality."

- "Father,
  you are as present and life-giving
  as my own heart.
  May each heartbeat I experience
  deepen my awareness of your presence."

- "Father,
  you embrace me as certainly
  as the clothes I wear.
  May each sensation I feel
  deepen my awareness of your loving embrace."

After having prayed one of the above prayers,
pause in a posture of openness to God's presence.
If God makes his presence felt,
as he does from time to time,
stay with it as long as it engages you prayerfully.

Do not be in a hurry to move on.
Some people meditate daily,
using only one of these exercises.
It helps them to seek a deeper level within themselves;
they merely spend the entire period of prayer
in a posture of openness to God.

Other ways to try to create
a "posture of openness" to God are the following:

Exhalation 1
"Lord, fill my mind with your light."
Inhalation 1
Picture light filling the mind.

Exhalation 2
"Fill my heart with your love."
Inhalation 2
Sense love filling the heart.

Exhalation 3
"Fill my body with your presence."
Inhalation 3
Feel the presence filling the body.

Repeat this prayerful rhythm 4 or 5 times.
Again, do not be in a hurry to move on.
A second way is this: pray mentally
and in rhythm with your breathing as follows:

Exhalation 1
"Lord, Jesus Christ,"
Inhalation 1
"Son of God,"

Exhalation 2
"Have mercy on me,"
Inhalation 2
"a sinner."

Again, repeat this cycle
as long as it engages you prayerfully.

Now experiment

During the coming week,
set aside 10–15 minutes daily for meditation.
The pages ahead contain meditation suggestions
for each day. Use this procedure:

1 Follow the pre-meditation steps just outlined.

2 When you have completed the last step,
   opening yourself to God's presence,
   turn to the meditation topic suggested.

3 Read the passage through once, slowly and
   prayerfully; pause and reflect upon it as a whole.

4 Reread the passage paragraph by paragraph,
   pausing and reflecting after each paragraph,
   so that if God wishes
   he may speak to you through it.

5 Conclude by speaking to God in your own words
   about how the passage applies to your own life.

Day one

When I was in Lebanon
I told some of my Arab friends
that I had loved a certain Arab proverb all my life.
An old man living in his mountain village
wrote it out in Arabic for me. . . . .

The proverb in English is:
"I will set my face to the wind
and scatter my handful of seed on high."

My little contribution to life. . .
is taken by the great wind of God and scattered
where the wind wants to scatter it. . . .
We need not bother too much about that part.
Seeds grow. But we must have the courage
to keep ourselves facing the wind. . . .

Peace and joy and fulfillment come
when we sow our seed,
and sometimes we see the harvest.
But even if we don't
other people do and they are grateful.
It is our gift to life and God.

Irene Champernowne
The One and Only Me

"What parable shall we use to explain it?
It is like a mustard seed. . . .
A man takes it and plants it in the ground;
after a while it grows up
and becomes the biggest of all plants.
It puts out such large branches
that the birds come and make their nests in its shade."

Mark 4:30–32

Day two

Geese don't get high-powered press coverage
like sea gulls.
They're seen as dull, ordinary birds
which only attract notice twice a year
during migration. . . .

Like the Blue Angels, they fly wing tip to wing tip. . .
you can hear the beat of their wings
whistling through the air in unison. . . .

And that's the secret of their strength. . . .
Together, cooperating as a flock,
geese can fly a 71-percent longer range. . . .
The lead goose cuts a swath
through the air resistance, which creates
a helping uplift for the two birds behind him.
In turn, their beating makes it easier on the birds
behind them, much like the drag of a race car
sucked in behind the lead car. . . .

Each bird takes his turn at being the leader.
The tired ones fan out to the edges of the V
for a breather, and the rested ones surge toward
the point of the V to drive the flock onward. . . .

If a goose becomes too exhausted or ill
and has to drop out of the flock,
he is never abandoned.
A stronger member of the flock will follow
the failing, weak one to his resting place
and wait until he's well enough to fly again.

Philip Yancey
"Benedict Arnold Seagull"

All of us . . .
have been baptized into the one body.

1 Corinthians 12:13

Day three

At the age of 7, Glenn Cunningham's legs
were so severely burned
that doctors considered amputation.
At the last minute they decided against it.
One of the doctors patted Glenn's shoulder:
"When the weather turns warm,
we'll get you into a chair on the porch."

"I don't want to sit.
I want to walk and run, and I will."
There was no doubt in Glenn's voice.
The doctor walked away.

Two years later, Glenn was running.
The boy was not running fast, but he was running.

Eventually, Glenn went to college.
His extracurricular activity was track.
No longer was he running to prove doctors wrong;
now he was running because he was good at it.
Soon intercollegiate records began to fall
under his driving legs.
Then came the Berlin Olympics.
Glenn not only qualified and ran in them,
but also broke the Olympic record
for the 1500-meter race.

The following year,
Glenn broke the world's indoor-mile record.
The boy who wasn't supposed to walk again
became the world's fastest human in the indoor mile.

Knock, and the door will be opened to you.
Matthew 7:7

Day four

The main trouble with Snoopy is
that he doesn't like being a dog.
He would much rather be a vulture, or a lion . . .
or a World War I flying ace.
He gets carried away by his fantasies.
One moment he's pretending to play golf. . . .
A moment later he might be dreaming
of being an Olympic speed skater. . . .

And all this time, of course,
he's lying on top of his doghouse,
while the real business of living
swirls about his feet.

It hardly needs to be said that these fantasies . . .
don't succeed in lifting him out of his dog's life.
The World War I flying ace
always falls victim to the dreaded Red Baron.
He invariably finds
that sitting in a tree like a vulture
is uncomfortable for his dog bottom,
and his lion imitation doesn't scare anyone. . . .

When troubled or worried. . .
he is apt to eat or sleep his problems away. . . .
Snoopy's chief aim in life, it seems,
is to be "off the hook. . . ."
He is an unashamed cop-out . . .
retreating into his fantasies
rather than taking up the responsibilities of life.

Don Brophy
"Morality According to Snoopy"

"If anyone wants to come with me,
he must forget himself, carry his cross,
and follow me."

Matthew 16:24

Day five

Research on army parachutists
has revealed an interesting truth:
Fear is highest for the novice jumper
at the moment he receives the "ready" signal
inside the airplane.
As he steps out of the plane
the prospective jumper has already reached
what has been called the "point of no return";
he has no place to go but down.

Strangely, it is at this very moment
that his fear begins to decrease.
In fact,
his fear lessens steadily during the free fall,
which is actually the time of greatest danger.

The researchers conclude
that the maximum amount of fear
usually occurs when the novice jumper realizes
that he is about to commit himself irrevocably
to a dangerous action.
As soon as this commitment is made,
the fear immediately begins to decline.

Eugene C. Kennedy
"You"

Jesus said:
"Aren't five sparrows sold for two pennies?
Yet not a single one of them is forgotten by God. . . .
So do not be afraid;
you are worth much more than many sparrows!"

Luke 12:6–7

Day six

Abraham Lincoln knew failure.
For 30 years it dogged his every footstep.
It walked the streets with him during the day.
It went to bed with him at night.

A partial list of his failures reads like this:

1832 defeated for the legislature
1833 failed in business
1836 nervous breakdown
1843 defeated in nomination for Congress
1854 defeated for Senate
1856 defeated in nomination for vice-president
1860 elected President

Lincoln was well prepared for the defeats and
setbacks that battered and bruised the nation
during the Civil War years.
Another man might have collapsed under the ordeal.

Of himself, Lincoln said:
"God selects his own instruments,
and sometimes they are queer ones;
for instance, he chose me
to steer the ship through a great crisis."

*What seems to be God's foolishness
is wiser than men's wisdom
and what seems to be God's weakness
is stronger than men's strength.*

1 Corinthians 1:25

Day seven

In *The Power and the Glory*, Graham Greene
tells of a priest who has been condemned to death
during an era of religious persecution in Mexico.
The terrifying tension of the priest's latter years
had driven him to drink:

*It was the morning of his death. He crouched
on the floor with the empty brandy flask in his hand
trying to remember an act of contrition.
"O God, I am sorry . . ."
He was confused . . . it was not the good death
for which one always prayed.*

*He caught sight of his own shadow on the cell wall. . . .
What a fool he had been to think that he
was strong enough to stay when others fled.
What an impossible fellow I am, he thought. . .
I have done nothing for anybody.
I might just as well have never lived. . . .*

*Tears poured down his face:
he was not at the moment afraid of damnation. . . .
He felt only an immense disappointment
because he had to go to God empty-handed,
with nothing at all.
It seemed to him at that moment
that it would have been quite easy
to have been a saint.
It would only have needed a little self-restraint
and a little courage.*

*He felt like someone who had missed happiness
by seconds at an appointed place.
He knew now that at the end
there was only one thing that counted—
to be a saint.*

2
You:
the
pray-er

In the scene

You see things vacationing on a motorcycle
in a way that is completely different from any other.
In a car you're always in a compartment,
and because you're used to it
you don't realize that through that car window
everything you see is just more TV.
You're a passive observer
and it is all moving by you boringly in a frame.

On a cycle the frame is gone.
You're completely in contact with it all.
You're in the scene, not just watching it anymore,
and the sense of presence is overwhelming.
That concrete
whizzing by five inches below your foot
is the real thing, the same stuff you walk on,
it's right there, so blurred you can't focus on it,
yet you can put your foot down and touch it anytime,
and the whole thing, the whole experience,
is never far removed from immediate consciousness.

Robert Pirsig
Zen and the Art of Motorcycle Maintenance

Prayer forms

Prayer is not too unlike vacationing on a motorcycle.
It gives you a different perspective of reality.
It introduces you to an old world in a new way.
You're *in* the scene.

Prayer normally takes one of 3 forms:

- meditation,

- contemplation,

- conversation.

Sometimes these 3 forms occur intertwined
in one and the same prayer—like strands of wire
coiled together in one and the same cable.

Meditation is thinking about God,
or seeking to become aware of God's action
or presence in your life.
God's presence in your life might be compared
to TV signals that are present everywhere.
Just as a TV set is needed
to bring the signals into focus,
so meditation is needed to bring into focus
God's presence and action in your life.

Meditation can be deliberately pursued.
That is, you can set the mood for meditation.
For example,
you can walk along a deserted beach
with the specific intention of thinking about God,
or life, or some problem that is vexing you.

Meditation can also take place unexpectedly.
Consider this incident:

One day after playing a hard game of basketball,
I went to a nearby fountain for some water.
The cool water tasted good,
and I felt refreshment enter my sore, tired body.
Suddenly, I began to think: we need water
for refreshment and strength.
"But where does water come from?" I wondered.
"Clouds," I thought.
"But where do clouds come from?"
"Vaporized air."
This went on until I got no answer.
Or rather, I was left with only one answer: God!

For the next couple of minutes,
I just lay on the grass, looking up into the sky,
marveling at what God must be like.

Then, I prayed to God (I forget what I said)
and started for home.

Contemplation is not so much seeking God
as marveling at God (as the boy did
toward the end of his experience).
In other words,
you are so struck by the idea of God
that you can hardly think or utter a word.
It is like enjoying a beautiful piece of music
or gazing spellbound at some fantastic view.

Conversation is the simplest form of prayer.
It is merely talking to God from the heart,
as the boy did at the end of his prayer.

In speaking of prayer, many people use the words
contemplation, meditation, and *conversation*
interchangeably.
Most spiritual directors, however,
tend to make this distinction:

meditation is thinking about God;
contemplation is resting in God;
and conversation is speaking to God.

Prayer styles

There are as many styles of prayer as there are
people who pray.
Some prayer styles, however, seem to have
a kind of universal appeal.

One such style is described by Ignatius of Loyola
in his *Spiritual Exercises.*
It consists merely of replaying in one's mind
and heart some episode,
either from the Bible or from popular literature.

The idea behind the technique
is to relive the event being described.
You don't stand outside the event as an observer.
You enter into it as an active participant.
You immerse yourself in what is happening,
experiencing it in all of its detail
with all five of your senses.

In other words,
you don't merely read about a blind man
being cured by Jesus. John 9:1-41
You actually become the blind man yourself.
You experience what he did
when he felt the fingers of Jesus
touch his eyes softly and gently.
You experience what he did
when he looked into the face of Jesus,
seeing another person for the first time in his life.

Ignatius' style of prayer is strikingly similar
to a reading technique described by Sydney Piddington
in "The Special Joys of Super-Slow Reading":

As I sat down on that hot and humid evening,
there seemed to be no solutions
to the problems thrashing around in my brain.
So I picked up a book,
settled into a comfortable chair
and applied my own special therapy—
super-slow reading.

I spent three hours on two short chapters
of Personal History by Vincent Sheean—
savoring each paragraph, lingering over
a sentence, a phrase, or even a single word,
building a detailed mental picture of the scene. . . .
Relishing every word,
I joined foreign correspondent Sheean
on a mission to China and another to Russia.
I lost myself in the author's world,
living his book.
And when finally I put it down,
my mind was totally refreshed.

I discovered its worth years ago,
in the infamous Changeli prisoner-of-war camp
in Singapore.
I was 19, an artillery sergeant,
when the city fell to the Japanese. . . .
Waiting with other Australian POWs,
I stuffed into my pack a copy of Lin Yutang's
The Importance of Living. . . .

Finally, as the sun went down one evening,
I walked out into the prison yard,
sat down on a pile of wood and,
under the glare of prison lights,
slowly opened the book to the title page
and frontispiece.

I spent three sessions on the preface,
then two whole evenings on the contents pages—
three and a half pages of chapter headings
with fascinating subtitles—
before I even reached page one. . . .

I started with the practical object
of making my book last.
But by the end of the second week,
still only on page ten,
I began to realize how much
I was getting from super-slow reading itself.
Sometimes just a particular phrase
caught my attention, sometimes a sentence.
I would read it slowly, analyze it, read it again—
perhaps changing down into an even lower gear—
and then sit for 20 minutes thinking about it
before moving on. . . .

The realization dawned on me that,
although my body was captive,
my mind was free to roam the world.
From Changeli,
I sailed with William Albert Robinson,
through his book Deep Water and Shoal.
In my crowded cell at night, lying on a concrete floor,
I felt myself dropping off to sleep in a warm cabin.
Next day, I'd be on deck again in a storm,
and after two or three graphic paragraphs
I'd be gripping the helm myself,
with the roar of the wind in my ears,
my hair thick with salt.

Super-slow reading complements perfectly
what Ignatius of Loyola says about contemplation.
He instructs his students
to make themselves physically present
at the gospel event they wish to contemplate.
In other words,
they are to experience in their imaginations
the sights, sounds, and feelings
that are described in the event.

Contemplation illustrated

I set a mood of prayer (e.g., breathing exercise)
and recall God's presence (e.g., breathing prayer).

Then, I *read* reflectively
the gospel event that I wish to contemplate:

*At noon
the whole country was covered with darkness,
which lasted for three hours.
At three o'clock Jesus cried out with a loud shout,
"Eloi, Eloi, lema sabachthani?"
which means,
"My God, my God, why did you abandon me?"*

*Some of the people who were there heard him
and said,
"Listen, he is calling for Elijah!"
One of them ran up with a sponge, soaked it in cheap wine,
and put it on the end of a stick.
Then he held it up to Jesus' lips and said,
"Wait! Let us see if Elijah
is coming to bring him down from the cross!"*

*With a loud cry Jesus died. . . .
The army officer, who was standing there in front
of the cross, saw how Jesus had cried out and died.
"This man was really the Son of God!" he said.*

Mark 15:33–39

step two

I *picture*, briefly,
the place where the gospel event takes place.
In this case, I see the hill of Calvary, near one of
the main roads outside the walled city of Jerusalem.

step three

I *ask* for some grace related to the gospel event.
In this case, I might ask for a deeper appreciation
of Jesus' love for me.

point one

I imagine I am one of the 20 or 30 Roman soldiers
on duty at the execution site. What do I see?

Hundreds of people milling about on Calvary—
some concerned, others merely curious.
Three men—stripped, bloody, gasping for breath—
hanging awkwardly on crosses.
The sky growing darker and darker.
Flashes of lightning. Swirling black clouds.
Excited birds, wheeling overhead and dipping down
into the crowd to pick up fallen particles of food.

point two

What do I smell?

The scent of rain in the air.
Sweaty bodies and sweat-soaked clothes.
Wine and dried fish—hawked by opportunist vendors.
The smell of blowing dust.

point three

What do I feel?

The air growing cooler. Perhaps a few raindrops.
Blowing sand, stinging my face and blinding
my eyes.

point four

What do I taste?

Salt and dust on my sun-parched lips.
Lukewarm water from a vendor's waterskin.

point five

What do I hear?

People cursing, laughing, crying, shouting.
Claps of thunder. Cries of birds circling overhead.
Jesus' voice: he cries out and the crowd grows still.
The Roman soldier's awed voice:
"This man was really the Son of God."

conclusion

What thoughts go through my mind
as I look at Jesus just before he dies—
and he looks directly at me?
I remain there, just looking at Jesus—and he at me.
I end by speaking to Jesus in my own words.

Now experiment

The pages ahead contain 7 meditation exercises
for each of the next 7 days.
Devote 10 to 15 minutes to each exercise.

Based on your meditation experiences of last week,
use whatever time, place, posture, or preparation
for meditation that you found worked best for you.
Or you may wish to continue experiments with these
during the coming week.

Use this procedure in pondering the meditation
material suggested:

1 Begin your meditation, following the steps
  outlined in the opening chapter.

2 When you complete the last step,
  opening yourself to God's presence,
  turn to the meditation topic suggested.

3 Put yourself "in the scene"
  and relive it, paragraph by paragraph,
  using all 5 of your senses.

4 End by speaking to God in your own words
  about how the topic applies to your life.

Day one

It happened to me in Cleveland.
What little I know of death and resurrection
I learned from Eastern Airlines.
It was the moment we dread . . .
whether we are seasoned travelers or not.
The moment when the captain's voice says,
cool, detached, distant as death,
". . . emergency . . . mechanical difficulty . . .
prepare . . . be calm."

I was terrified.
We had twenty minutes . . .
to watch the stewardess run through the drill again . . .
to fold the pillow on our laps . . .
to wait for—as they called it—impact.
Twenty minutes in which to remember how to pray.
Twenty minutes to live. Twenty minutes to die. . . .

What matters to me about Cleveland
and those twenty minutes, twelve, seven, three,
wheels down, impact,
is that I died, no matter what the papers said.
By the time that plane
came to a stop at the terminal, I was gone. . . .

I was gone and I came back.
Resurrection took flesh. My flesh.
Resurrection is what happens
when we survive what we had no right to.

If there is a promise in Cleveland,
it is that I who died live. . . .

And why? For what?

James Carroll
A Terrible Beauty

Day two

Thor Heyerdahl, the famous sea adventurer,
overcame his fear of water in his youth
when a canoe carrying him and 2 companions capsized.

When Thor surfaced,
he saw the capsized canoe racing toward the falls
and one of his companions groping for the shore.
Thor's heavy army clothes
were dragging him beneath the surface. . . .
He had a very clear thought that soon he would know
which one of his parents was right about
life after death. [His father said there was such a
life; his mother denied it.]

As the roar of the nearing falls grew louder,
the words of the Lord's Prayer
entered his mind and he prayed.
A sudden burst of will came with his prayer. . . .
He felt a presence greater than himself.
He began to keep pace with the rushing water.
Every time he thought of giving up,
a strange strength came back and he went on,
helped by something he could not see.

He realized a companion, Rulle, was clinging
to a tree limb and leaning over the water toward him.
He surged the last few inches to his friend's fingertips.
Then exhausted, Rulle and Thor
dragged a third comrade from the water. . . .

That day on the Oxtongue River,
Thor lost his fear of water. . . .
And he gained something else—
a sure knowledge that his father was right.

Lois Briener
"The Man Who Was Afraid of Water"

Day three

Others may describe the moon as barren
and desolate, and technically they are correct—
there is no water or air, no sound of life.
But, although a dead world, it can be a beautiful one
to anyone who loves the mountains of earth as I do.

When I first climbed down the ladder
of Apollo 15's lunar module,
I was taken aback that the mountains . . .
seemed so close and so tall. . . .
But the real surprise was that the mountains,
at first sight,
were not gray or brown, as I had expected.
They were golden. . . .

It seemed like a friendly place, which surprised me.
Here Dave Scott and I were on the moon,
strangers in a strange environment,
and you would have thought
we would have been a little lost.
But no, I felt that I was where I should be. . . .

Each night, when we bedded down in the lunar module,
I would lie awake a few minutes
and reflect on the beauty of what I had seen
and try to etch in my mind a lasting impression
of the majesty of those mountains. . . .

Running through my reflections
like the refrain of an old hymn were the words . . .
from Psalms [121]:
"I will lift up mine eyes unto the hills,
from whence cometh my help.
My help cometh from the Lord."

Col. James R. Irwin
"Apollo 15: Three Views of the Moon"

Day four

There were some shepherds
in that part of the country
who were spending the night in the fields,
taking care of their flocks.
An angel of the Lord appeared to them,
and the glory of the Lord shone over them.
They were terribly afraid,
but the angel said to them,

"Don't be afraid!
I am here with good news for you,
which will bring great joy to all the people.
This very day in David's town
your Savior was born—Christ the Lord!
What will prove it to you is this:
you will find a baby wrapped in cloths
and lying in a manger."

So they hurried off and found Mary and Joseph,
and saw the baby lying in the manger.
When the shepherds saw him they told them
what the angel had said about this child.
All who heard it were filled with wonder
at what the shepherds told them.

Mary remembered all these things
and thought deeply about them.

The shepherds went back, singing praises to God
for all they had heard and seen;
it had been just as the angel had told them.

Luke 2:8-20

Day five

Some men came
carrying a paralyzed man on a bed,
and they tried to take him into the house
and lay him before Jesus.
Because of the crowd, however,
they could find no way to take him in.

So they carried him up on the roof,
made an opening in the tiles,
and let him down on his bed
into the middle of the group in front of Jesus.

When Jesus saw how much faith they had,
he said to the man,
"Your sins are forgiven you, my friend."

The teachers of the Law and the Pharisees
began to say to themselves, "Who is this man
who speaks against God in this way?
No man can forgive sins; God alone can!"

Jesus knew their thoughts and said to them,
"Why do you think such things? Is it easier to say,
'Your sins are forgiven you,'
or to say, 'Get up and walk'?
I will prove to you, then, that the Son of Man
has authority on earth to forgive sins."

So he said to the paralyzed man,
"I tell you, get up, pick up your bed, and go home!"

At once the man got up before them all,
took the bed he had been lying on,
and went home, praising God.

Luke 5:18–25

Day six

On the evening of that same day
Jesus said to his disciples,
"Let us go across to the other side of the lake."

So they left the crowd;
the disciples got into the boat that Jesus
was already in, and took him with them.
Other boats were there too.

A very strong wind blew up
and the waves began to spill over into the boat,
so that it was about to fill with water.

Jesus was in the back of the boat,
sleeping with his head on a pillow.
The disciples woke him up and said,
"Teacher, don't you care that we are about to die?"

Jesus got up and commanded the wind,
"Be quiet!" and said to the waves, "Be still!"
The wind died down, and there was a great calm.

Then Jesus said to his disciples,
"Why are you frightened?
Are you still without faith?"
But they were terribly afraid,
and began to say to each other,
"Who is this man?
Even the wind and the waves obey him!"

Mark 4: 35–41

Day seven

He was encased in a plaster cast
when they brought him to [prison] . . .
and as we watched
he pushed a hand into the breast of thin grey shell
and extracted a small tattered book.
None of us had seen a book of any kind for years.
Avram lay there quietly turning the pages,
until he became conscious of the eager eyes
fixed on him.

"Your book," I said,
"What is it? Where did you get it?"

"It's the Gospel according to St. John. . . .
I managed to hide it in my cast
when the police came for me."
He smiled. "Would you like to borrow it?"

I took the little book in my hands
as if it were a live bird. No life-saving drug
could have been more precious to me. . . .

The Gospel went from hand to hand.
It was difficult to give up. . . .

Many learned the Gospel by heart
and we discussed it every day among ourselves.

Richard Wurmbrand
In God's Underground

John writes:
These things have been written
that you may believe
that Jesus is the Messiah, the Son of God,
and that through this faith
you may have life in his name.

John 20: 31

He changed

Hoodlums killed his father,
and his mother went insane caring for the family.
No wonder "Big Red" ended up in prison.
Yet, when he died,
Raymond Schroth wrote in *America* magazine:

Now he is dust. . . .
Yet, in a quick, tragic existence
he achieved in heroic manner
what society usually credits to sages and saints:
he had changed.
He had come to know, without flinching,
the evil in himself and in the world.
He had opened his soul—pock-marked as it was—
enough to cleanse it and to glimpse
his own limitations and the previously invisible bonds
that linked him to all men of all classes and colors.
"Malcolm X Is Alive"

Spiritual reading

What transformed this man
from a common criminal into a social reformer?
"Big Red's" own autobiography
suggests a partial answer:

*Not long ago, an English writer telephoned me
from London, asking questions.
One was, "What's your alma mater?"
I told him, "Books."...
Every time I catch a plane,
I have a book with me that I want to read....
I could spend the rest of my life reading,
just satisfying my curiosity.*

Malcolm X, asst. Alex Haley
Autobiography of Malcolm X

In his *Autobiography*, Malcolm X leaves us
a description of his program of study in prison:

*Many...
think I went to school far beyond the eighth grade.
This impression is due entirely to my prison studies....*

*[In prison] every book I picked up
had a few sentences which...
might as well have been in Chinese.
When I just skipped those words, of course,
I really ended up with little idea
of what the book said....*

*I saw that the best thing I could do
was to get hold of a dictionary—
to study, to learn some words....*

No university
would ask any student to devour literature as I did
when this new world opened up to me,
of being able to read and understand. . . .

When I had progressed to really serious reading,
every night at about ten p.m.
I would be outraged with the "lights out. . . ."

Fortunately, right outside my door
was a corridor light that cast a glow into my room.
The glow was enough to read by,
once my eyes adjusted to it.
So when "lights out" came, I would sit on the floor
where I could continue my reading in that glow.

At one-hour intervals the night guards
paced past every room.
Each time I heard the approaching footsteps,
I jumped into bed and feigned sleep.
And as soon as the guard passed, I got back out
of bed onto the floor area of that light-glow,
where I would read for another fifty-eight minutes—
until the guard approached again.
That went on until three or four every morning.

Spiritual directors have always assigned
a significant place to reading
in the development of the spiritual life of people.

Teresa of Avila, the Carmelite mystic,
often went to prayer with a book in her hand.
At one stage of her life she wrote:

Often the mere fact that I had it by me was enough.
Sometimes I read a little, sometimes a great deal.

Spiritual reading normally takes one of 4 forms:

- instructional: teaching about prayer
  in particular
  and the spiritual life in general,

- inspirational: encouraging growth
  in prayer and the spiritual life,

- pre-prayer: serving as a preparation
  for prayer,

- meditative: acting as a guide
  during prayer.

In choosing a book for spiritual reading,
it will be helpful to consult someone you feel
will be a competent advisor.

A book that is too theological
or too spiritually advanced
could defeat the purpose of spiritual reading.
Confusion about the spiritual life, in general,
or prayer, in particular, could result.

Now, let's take a closer look at the various kinds
of spiritual reading.

Instructional reading

Zen Buddhist monks will tell you
that they sit in meditation morning and evening,
but that Zen is not just that. Zen is walking,
Zen is working, Zen is eating, Zen is life.

That is to say,
the interior solitude found in the sitting exercise
known as zazen is maintained all during the day.
And if one has the good fortune
to reach enlightenment,
this liberating moment will generally come
not in time of meditation but quite unexpectedly
at the falling of a peach blossom
or the sound of the temple bell.

Now a Christian contemplative life
runs parallel with this,
even though its content is vastly different.
One prays morning and evening
as part of the rhythm of life.
But contemplation is not just this.
Rather it is an enduring state of openness
to the voice of God. . . .

Like Zen, contemplation is walking, sitting,
working, eating, and so on;
and quite often the greatest inspirations
will come not in time of formal prayer . . .
they may come through conversations with others,
through reading the Bible,
through disappointments, through suffering.

When this openness is maintained,
life becomes an experience of God.

William Johnston
"Religious Life: Contemplative Life"

Another example of "instructional" reading is
Joseph Grassi's "Meditation: What? Why? How?"
Here are some meditation suggestions from it:

Select a quality or characteristic of Christ
that you would like to see as part of your life,
such as patience.
Recall or search the Gospels
for Jesus' words about this virtue. . . .
Let your mind dwell on the times in Christ's life
when he showed patience, as in the agony
in the garden or the suffering on the cross.
Then let your heart freely admire this quality
of Christ's and express your love
for the person who so exemplified it. . . .
End your meditation
with the resolution to practice the virtue
and a prayer for strength to be able to do so. . . .

Pick up a book of the Bible that you wish to use
for a series of daily readings over a period of time.
Slowly read a passage—out loud if possible.
Then remain in silence for a few minutes,
quietly allowing anything to come to mind
that is freely associated with the reading.
Make a special note of any insight that affects your life.
When you feel ready,
take another reading and repeat the process.

As you reflect on the reading,
imagine you are one of the characters in the story,
possibly Moses on Mt. Sinai.
In this case you would climb the mountain with him
and try to really feel
the effect of hearing the actual voice of God.

Inspirational reading

A second kind of spiritual reading
is "inspirational" reading.
An example is this excerpt from "The Presidency"
by Hugh Sidey:

Men who have served in the Presidency
have often found that their faiths . . .
take on new meaning once they gain the Oval Office.
As World War I closed in on the United States,
Woodrow Wilson astounded his Cabinet
by kneeling before them in prayer. . . .

John F. Kennedy's regular attendance at Mass
and his skillful use of Scripture in his orations
seemed in his campaign
and the early months of his Presidency
designed more to please the voters than himself.
But after the Bay of Pigs, the Berlin crunch
and the Cuban missile crisis,
anyone close to Kennedy could detect a change
in his views of spiritual matters.
He became less public
and more private about them.

On one of those quiet evenings in the Oval Office
when the day's clamor had faded,
not long before he was killed,
he sat behind his desk and for a few silent seconds
gazed through the bullet-proof windows.
Then he nodded an admission
that God was more important in the scheme of things
than he at one time had sensed.
But when asked to talk about it he refused.
That, he said,
was something he intended to keep to himself.

A second example of inspirational reading
is this excerpt from
Dawn Without Darkness by Anthony Padovano:

The man who prays pushes hope
into areas where men who never dream
never venture. . . .

Unless one prays,
he is likely to dream not at all
or to dream only
of what shall actually come to pass,
or to dream only what is humanly possible.
Hence God, who is not humanly possible,
becomes unreal;
providence is dismissed as magic,
heaven as medieval, hope as wishful thinking. . . .

Prayer reaches our lives
as we begin to do things we could not have done
unless we had prayed.
We begin to believe,
we seek forgiveness,
we love those who would otherwise
have been unlovable to us. . . .
Prayer is not a pious addition to things. . . .
It is a force allowing things to happen
which could not have occurred without it.
Jesus could not have gone to the cross
unless he had first prayed in Gethsemane.

A final example of inspirational reading
is this excerpt from *Prayer and Hope* by Henri Nouwen:

The man who prays with hope . . .
might ask for everything . . .
like nice weather or an advancement.
This concreteness is even a sign of authenticity.
For if you ask only for faith, hope, love . . .
without making them concrete in the nitty-gritty
of life,
you probably haven't involved God in your real life.

But if you pray with hope,
all those concrete requests are merely . . .
ways of saying
that we trust in the fullness of God's goodness. . . .
Whenever we pray with hope,
we put our lives in the hands of God.
Fear and anxiety fade away,
and everything we are given
and everything we are deprived of
is nothing but a finger
pointing out the direction of God's hidden promise
which we shall taste in full.

Pre-prayer reading

Another type of spiritual reading is "pre-prayer" reading.

Its purpose is to serve as a point of departure for prayer.

Here's an example from *The Allelulia Affair* by Malcolm Boyd:

Jesus pulled his legs free.
The rusty nails that held his feet captive
fell clanking below the cross.

It was not difficult now to free his left hand,
then the right one.
He slid easily down from the full-size wooden
cross in the sanctuary
of an inner-city church in Indianapolis.

Next he walked into the adjoining parish hall.
He passed by Catherine Coombs of the altar guild
who fainted.
Jesus washed in the men's room—
he got the blood off his body—and left the building,
walking toward the city's hub, Monument Circle.

It was a hot day, so he felt okay in his loincloth.

Jesus had a bit more difficulty disengaging
himself from a gold processional cross
in an East Side church in Manhattan,
yet within just a few moments he was free. . . .

[Jesus] headed south toward Rockefeller Center.
A cab driver moving along Madison Avenue . . .
saw Jesus, who was still wearing
his crown of thorns.
Before he knew what he was doing,
the driver had smashed his cab into the plate-
glass window of an art gallery. . . .

It was inside a church in Moscow
that an altogether new phenomenon . . .
was first observed.

Katerina Palov
had been absorbed in her private devotions
inside the Moscow church.

Now she looked toward a cross. . . .
But to her amazement . . .
Katerina discovered that a young black man
was firmly nailed to the wood.

He did not look like Jesus.
He was fully dressed
in some kind of a striped uniform.

Investigators discovered
that the young black man on the cross
was a convict who was serving forty years
in a South African prison. . . .

It was 3:45 p.m. when Clara Morris
stopped off for a moment of prayer in a church
on Wilshire Boulevard in Los Angeles.

She was startled to see a body upon a cross,
for she was aware that now all crosses
were empty.

Drawing close, she saw a brown woman
and heard her crying.

The woman was identified as an "Untouchable"
who lived in Bombay.

Twelve hours later inside a church
in Addis Ababa, a white youth was found
nailed to an altar cross
that had previously borne Jesus.

The youth told the Ethiopian Red Cross
that he lived in Evanston, Illinois. . . .

There were scars of beatings on his body
and his left eye was swollen shut.

So people began to see.

Concerning pre-prayer reading,
the amount that you read is not really important.
A few sentences or paragraphs
may be enough to move you to prayer.
Or it may be necessary to read several pages.
A lot depends upon how you happen to feel at the time.

One final point.
You should perform your pre-prayer reading slowly
and attentively—not rapidly or casually,
as you might read the evening newspaper.
When your attention focuses sufficiently
and you are moved to a spirit of prayer,
close the book and set it aside.
It has served its purpose.

Meditative reading

Reading can also act as a guide during prayer.
A renowned spiritual director, Francis de Sales,
gives this advice in one of his letters:

Do not become discouraged,
if sometimes, and even quite often,
you do not find consolation in your meditation.
Persevere at it with patience and humility. . . .
Make use of your books, when you grow weary.
That is, read a little and then meditate.
Keep this up until the end of your prayer.

This method of praying is sometimes called
"meditative" reading. It involves 3 simple steps:

• reading a line or phrase at a time,

• applying it to your life,

• speaking to God about it.

The book or material you select for meditative
reading should be rich in content:
a passage from Scripture,
an inspirational prayer or poem,
a provocative selection from a novel or essay.

The important thing about meditative reading
is not the reading but the dialogue with Jesus
or the Father that flows out of the reading.

To get an idea of how meditative reading works,
consider Ignatius' "Prayer for Generosity":

Lord, teach me to be generous.
Teach me to serve you as you deserve;
>   *to give and not to count the cost;*
>   *to fight and not to heed the wounds;*
>   *to toil and not to seek for rest;*
>   *to labor and not to ask for reward,*
except to know that I am doing your will.

Now let us apply the principles of meditative reading to the prayer:

- Lord, teach me to be generous.

Generosity is not my strong point, Lord.
Teach me to become like the widow in the Gospel.
You said to her:
"The others put in what they had to spare . . .
but she . . . put in all she had."
Mark 12:44

- to serve you as you deserve;

Lord, I must be honest. I rarely think of my life
as being one of service to you.
Help me to start taking to heart your words:
"No servant can be the slave of two masters."
Luke 16:13

- to give and not to count the cost;

The widow did this; how different from me, Lord!
I'm always counting the cost. Lord, someone said:
"Who gives quickly, gives twice."
Help me to start giving twice.

- to fight and not to heed the wounds;

That's what the early Christians did.
Lord, when I panic, remind me of their words:
"We hang on crosses, we are licked by flames,
the sword lays open our throat, the wild beast
springs upon us. . . . To do great things is Roman,
to suffer great things is Christian." (Tertullian)

- to toil and not to seek for rest;

This is what Jesus did throughout his life.
Lord, when I grow tired and seek for rest,
remind me of your own words:
"Come to me, all of you who are tired. . . .
Learn from me."
Matthew 11:28-29

- to labor and not to ask for reward;

It is so easy to fall into the rut of working for rewards:
praise from others or money.
Lord, help me to begin to live by your words:
"Your Father, who sees what you do in private,
will reward you."
Matthew 6:18

- except to know that I am doing your will.

"Thy will be done!" I say these words of the Lord's
Prayer every day. I want to begin to live them.
"Father . . . not my will . . .
but your will be done."
Luke 22:42

Now experiment

The matter for the next 7 days of meditation
will be prayers composed by famous Christians.
The method of meditation
will be that of meditative reading.
The procedure is as follows:

- reading a line or phrase at a time,

- applying it to your life,

- speaking to God/Jesus about it.

Devote from 10 to 15 minutes to each exercise.
Do not forget the pre-meditation steps,
as outlined in the first chapter.

Day one

During his youth,
St. Augustine lived a seriously disordered life.
Moved by the preaching of St. Ambrose,
Augustine underwent a radical conversion in 387.
His autobiographical work, *The Confessions*,
contains this prayer:

Late have I loved you,
O beauty ever ancient, ever new!
Late have I loved you.

And behold, you were within,
and I without,
and without I sought you.
And deformed,
I ran after those forms of beauty
you have made.

You were with me,
and I was not with you,
those things held me back from you,
things whose only being
was to be in you.

You called; you cried;
and you broke through my deafness.
You flashed; you shone;
and you chased away my blindness.
You became fragrant;
and I inhaled and sighed for you.
I tasted,
and now hunger and thirst for you.
You touched me;
and I burned for your embrace.

Day two

Morris West wrote of John XXIII in *Life:*
"Will they canonize him
and make him, officially, a saint in the calendar?
In a way I hope not. . . .
I want to remember him for what he was—
a loving man, a simple priest,
a good pastor and a builder of bridges
across which we poor devils may hope one day
to scramble to salvation."
Shortly before his death, John composed a prayer:

O Lord,
do not let us turn into "broken cisterns,"
that can hold no water . . .
do not let us be so blinded by the enjoyment
of the good things of earth
that our hearts become insensible to the cry
of the poor,
of the sick,
of orphaned children
and of those innumerable brothers of ours
who lack the necessary minimum
to eat, to cloth their nakedness,
and to gather their family together under one roof.

Pope John XXIII
Journal of a Soul

"Come and receive the kingdom. . . .
I was hungry and you fed me,
thirsty and you gave me drink;
I was a stranger and you received me . . .
naked and you clothed me;
I was sick and you took care of me,
in prison and you visited me."

Matthew 25:34–36

Day three

Jerome
began his career living in solitude in the desert.
In A.D. 382, he set out to preach the Gospel
to others.

The final years of his life were spent in a cave
in Bethlehem, translating the Bible into Latin,
which was the language of the common people
in his time.

About 120 of Jerome's personal letters remain to us;
one is stained with his own tears.
Here's a prayer that Jerome composed:

Show me, O Lord, your mercy,
and delight my heart with it.
Let me find you,
whom so lovingly I seek.

See, here is the man
whom the robbers seized and manhandled,
and left half-dead on the road to Jericho.
You can do what the kindly Samaritan could not do.
Come to my aid!

I am the sheep
who wandered off into the wilderness.
Look for me,
and bring me back home to your fold.

Do with me whatever you will,
that I may be with you all the days of my life,
and praise you,
in the company of all your friends for ever.

Day four

In his *Apologia*, John Henry Newman says
that as a boy he often read the Bible.
He also says that the writings of Augustine and
Ambrose affected his thinking deeply.

After meditating on the changes and fortunes
of life, he wrote this prayer:

All below heaven changes:
spring,
summer,
autumn,
each has its turn.

The fortunes of the world change;
what was high, lies low;
what was low, lies high.
Riches take wing and flee;
bereavements happen.
Friends become enemies,
and enemies friends.
Our wishes, aims, and plans
change.

There is nothing stable,
but you, O my God!
And you are the center and life of all
who change,
who trust you as their Father,
who look to you
and are content to put themselves
into your hands.

Day five

Orphaned at 16,
Tom Merton became a communist at the age of 20.
At 23 he found Christ,
and at 24 he became a *New York Times* reporter.
Two years later, with all he owned in a duffel bag,
he entered a Trappist monastery in Kentucky.
He remained there until his death in 1969.
Merton leaves a record of his journey toward faith
in this prayer:

My Lord God,
I have no idea where I am going.
I do not see the road ahead of me.
I cannot know for certain where it will end.

Nor do I really know myself,
and the fact that I think
that I am following your will
does not mean that I am actually doing so.
But I believe that the desire to please you
does in fact please you.
And I hope that I have that desire
in all that I am doing.
I hope that I will never do anything
apart from that desire.
And I know that if I do this
you will lead me by the right road
though I may know nothing about it.

Therefore will I trust you always
though I may seem to be lost
and in the shadow of death.
I will not fear, for you are ever with me,
and will never leave me to face my perils alone.

Thoughts in Solitude

Day six

To live more as Jesus did, Francis of Assisi
turned his back on his family's wealth.
Followers flocked to the charismatic youth,
and the Franciscan order was born.
Here's a prayer that Francis composed
before he died in 1226:

*Lord,
make me an instrument of your peace.*

*Where there is hatred,
let me sow love;
where there is injury,
pardon;
where there is doubt,
faith;
where there is despair,
hope;
where there is darkness,
light;
and where there is sadness,
joy.*

*Grant that I may not so much
seek to be consoled as to console;
to be understood as to understand;
to be loved as to love;*

*for it is in giving
that we receive;
it is in pardoning
that we are pardoned;
and it is in dying
that we are born into eternal life.*

Day seven

An 11th-century monk,
Anselm of Canterbury, wrote a deeply personal,
almost intimate, book called *Proslogion*.
It was designed to help the unlearned to find God.
The book contains this prayer:

O Lord my God,
teach my heart where and how to seek you,
where and how to find you. . . .

O Lord,
you are my God
and you are my Lord,
and I have never seen you.

You have made me and remade me,
and you have bestowed on me
all the good things I possess,
and still I do not know you. . . .
I have not yet done that
for which I was made. . . .

Teach me to seek you . . .
for I cannot seek you
unless you teach me
or find you
unless you show yourself to me.

Let me seek you in my desire,
let me desire you in my seeking.
Let me find you by loving you,
let me love you when I find you.

4
You:
the
chronicler

Personal journal

In *The Secret of Staying in Love,*
John Powell writes:

Most of us think that we are better speakers
than writers, which may be true. . . .
However, I would like to put in a strong word
of encouragement for doing at least some writing,
especially in the beginning and during the critical
times of a love-relationship. . . .

So find yourself a notebook, a pen,
and begin now with your partner in dialogue
to discover for yourselves
what sharing can mean to a love-relationship.

On the following pages
you will find 40 suggested entry-topics.
It is recommended that you take one each day.
Read over the questions given there.
Then listen to your own answers and emotional
reactions.
Try to verbalize these as vividly as possible
in your journal.

Now begin

Here are some typical entry-topics
suggested by Powell:

ten statement autobiography

If anyone were to understand in depth the real you,
what are the ten most essential things
he would have to know about you?
In these ten statements please do not include
any obvious external facts
which are visible to all who know you.
Rather they should reveal the person under all the
costumes and roles, his deepest reality
as opposed to his surface appearance.
For example,
"I have always been afraid of the opposite sex. . . .
The turning point of my whole life
was my mother's death."

strongest recent emotion

In the past six months or year of your life,
what was your deepest and strongest emotion?
If there were several, just pick any one.
Record something of the occasion and circumstances
of stimulation
but mostly describe the feeling as vividly as you can.

the future

Describe your predominant emotional reaction
to your anticipated future.
Are you eager
for the future or afraid of the uncertainties?
Do you dread the things that you see as inevitable?

Calculate as best you can where you will be
and what you will be doing in five years, in ten years.
Is the prospect
frightening, boring, dreadful or delightful?
What do you feel about who will decide your future?
Do you have a feeling of being in control of your life?

death

In your imagination see yourself on your deathbed.
The doctor says that it will be only a matter of hours.
How would you feel?
Describe whatever fears, regrets, satisfactions,
peace, panic, or hopes might come to you. . . .
Do you repress or look away from the thought
of dying? . . .
Does the thought of or belief in an afterlife actively
influence your emotional reactions to dying?

entry from a college student's journal

"If I had only a short time to live, I would
immediately contact all the people
I had ever really loved,
and I'd make sure they knew I had really loved them.
Then I would play all the records that meant most
to me, and I would sing all my favorite songs.
And oh I would dance. I would dance all night.
I would look at my blue skies and feel my warm
sunshine. I would tell the moon and the stars
how lovely and beautiful they are.
I would say 'goodbye' to all the little things I own,
my clothes, my books and my 'stuff.'
Then I would thank God for the great gift of life,
and die in his arms."

Personal prayer journal

A young man told me that he had decided to give up
the program of meditation
which he had begun about 4 months earlier.
(He had not meditated for over 2 weeks.)
Then, quite by accident,
while looking for something else,
he happened to come across his Prayer Journal.
He stopped what he was doing and began to read it.

"Reading from my Journal," said the young man,
"inspired me to begin meditating again.
If it hadn't been for it, I wouldn't be praying today."

It is for reasons like this
that spiritual directors have always recommended
the use of Prayer Journals for beginners.
It is not necessary to write in it every day.
In fact, it may even be better
to restrict your entries to 2 or 3 times a week.
The only way to find out what works best for you
is to experiment.

A personal Prayer Journal is merely a notebook
in which you record insights
and reflections concerning your spiritual life,
especially your experiences in prayer.

Perhaps one of the best-known Prayer Journals
is Pope John XXIII's *Journal of a Soul.*
"My soul is in these pages," said Pope John
as he turned over his spiritual notes,
shortly before he died.

The journals spanned almost 67 years.
The last entry was penned 6 months before death.
Here are some excerpts:

I find I am still at the very beginning
of the journey which I have undertaken. . . .
I thought I could have been a saint by this time,
and instead I am still as miserable as before.
April 4, 1896

The other evening I had no candle,
last night I had no ink,
and so for two evenings running
I have written nothing. . . .
I am still stuck in the same place,
without moving a step forward.
August 12, 1898

Every evening from the window of my room . . .
I see an assemblage of boats on the Bosporus;
they come round from the Golden Horn
in tens and hundreds . . . a most impressive
spectacle of colour and lights. . . .
These lights glow all night
and one can hear the cheerful voices of fishermen.
I find the sight very moving.
The other night, towards one o'clock,
it was pouring rain
but the fishermen were still there,
undeterred from their heavy toil. . . .

Very little is left in this land
of the kingdom of Jesus Christ.
Debris and seeds. . . .
We must do as the fishermen of the Bosporus do,
work night and day.
Istanbul, 1939

I must not disguise from myself the truth:
I am definitely approaching old age.
My mind resents this and almost rebels,
for I still feel so young, eager, agile, alert.
But one look in my mirror disillusions me.
This is the season of maturity . . .
perhaps the time granted to me for living
is brief. . . .
This thought caused Hezekiah to turn to the wall
and weep. I do not weep.

No, I do not weep, and I do not even desire
to live my life over again, so as to do better.
I entrust to the Lord's mercy
whatever I have done, badly or less than well.
France, 1945

I feel I have no longer any special ties in this life,
no family, no earthly country or nation. . . .
The whole world is my family.
Retreat notes (as pope), 1959

Israel's prayer journal

The most famous Prayer Journal of all times
is the Book of Psalms.
More than any other book of the Bible,
it allows us to glimpse the soul of the Israelite.
We see how he talks to God in times of deep doubt,
depression, and joy. Here are some examples:

I am gripped by fear and trembling;
I am overcome with horror.
I say, "I wish I had wings, like a dove!"
I would fly away . . .
and make my home in the desert.
I would hurry and find myself a shelter
from the raging wind and the storm.
55:1, 5–8

How happy are those whose strength
comes from you. . . .
As they pass through the dry valley
it becomes like a place of springs;
the early rain fills it with pools.
They grow stronger as they go.
84:5–7

In graphic images like these,
the Book of Psalms puts us in touch with the deeper
beliefs and feelings of the Israelite people.

Because they are prayerful expressions,
the psalms do not always yield their treasure readily.
They resist the hurried observer
and open themselves only to the reflective "pray-er."

Jesus' prayer journal

Jesus wrote no Prayer Journal of his own,
but the evangelists have preserved for us a kind of
"Prayer Journal of Jesus" in the Gospel.
For example, near the end of his public ministry,
this prayer of Jesus is found:

*"Father, Lord of heaven and earth! I thank you
because you have shown to the unlearned
what you have hidden from the wise and learned.
Yes, Father,
this was done by your own choice and pleasure."*
Luke 10:21

At the Last Supper, Jesus prayed:

*"Father, the hour has come. . . .
I have made you known to the men you gave me. . . .
I pray that they may all be one. Father!
May they be in us,
just as you are in me and I am in you.
May they be one,
so that the world will believe that you sent me."*
John 17:1–21

In the garden, Jesus prayed:

*"Father . . . if you will, take this cup away from me.
Not my will, however, but your will be done."*
Luke 22:42

On the cross:

*"Forgive them, Father!
They don't know what they are doing."*
Luke 23:34

"Father! In your hands I place my spirit!"
Luke 23:46

Now experiment

The matter for the next 7 days of meditation
will be passages taken from Israel's Prayer Journal,
the Book of Psalms. Use the following procedure:

- read a line or two,

- reflect upon it prayerfully,

- speak to God about it.

Take an extra minute after each daily meditation
to jot down
any significant reflections upon your prayer.
The entry in your Prayer Journal may read
something like this:

March 11
9:30 p.m.   After showering this morning,
I meditated cross-legged,
my back tight against the wall.
I'm getting used to this position.
It really seems to work.
I meditated on Psalm 46.
It made me reflect on my own fighting
in our family.
I resolved to try to change things,
but I realize it won't be easy.
Nonetheless, I will try.

Day one

While hiding from enemies in the hills and caves
of Judah, David composed Psalm 63.
If it helps you to pray, picture yourself as David,
who used to pray the psalm to God under night skies:

God, you are my God,
and I long for you.
My whole being desires you;
my soul is thirsty for you,
like a dry, worn-out, and waterless land.
Let me see you in the sanctuary;
let me see how mighty and glorious you are.

Your constant love is better than life itself,
and so I praise you.
I will give thanks to you as long as I live;
I will raise my hands to you in prayer. . . .

As I lie in bed I remember you;
all night long I think of you,
because you have always been my help.
In the shadow of your wings I sing for joy.
I cling to you
and your hand keeps me safe.

Day two

George Cornell said of American prisoners
returned from the tragic war in Vietnam:

"PWs told of setting up worship services . . .
and conducting Bible studies—often from memory—
at most PW camps."

Psalm 23 was the "most frequently used" psalm.
If it helps, picture yourself as one of the PWs,
praying the psalm during a prison worship service:

The Lord is my shepherd;
I have everything I need.
He lets me rest in fields of green grass
and leads me to quiet pools of fresh water.
He gives me new strength.

He guides me in the right way,
as he promised.
Even if that way goes through deepest darkness,
I will not be afraid, Lord,
Your shepherd's rod and staff keep me safe.

You prepare a banquet for me,
where all my enemies can see me;
you welcome me by pouring ointment on my head
and fill my cup to the brim.
Certainly your goodness and love
will be with me as long as I live;
and your house will be my home forever.

Day three

One of the saddest but most inspiring dramas
of American history
took place at Valley Forge in the winter of 1777.
French General Lafayette, who had just joined the
staff of Washington, wrote:

"The unfortunate soldiers were in want of everything.
The army frequently went whole days without food;
and the patient endurance of soldiers and officers
was a miracle."

When he accepted command of the American
Revolutionary Forces, Washington prayed Psalm 101:

My song is about loyalty and justice,
and I sing it to you, Lord.
My conduct will be faultless. . . .
I will never tolerate evil. . . .

I hate the actions of those who turn away from God;
I will have nothing to do with them.
I will not be dishonest. . . .

I will approve of those who are faithful to God
and let them live in my palace;
those who are completely honest
will be allowed to serve me.

No liar will live in my palace;
no hypocrite will remain in my presence. . . .
I will expel all evil men from the city of the Lord.

Day four

Psalm 46 inspired Martin Luther's
"A Mighty Fortress Is Our God."

The same psalm inspired Isaac Watts'
"O God Our Help in Ages Past."

President Eisenhower, also, chose this psalm
for his preinaugural worship, January 20, 1957.

God is our shelter and strength,
always ready to help in times of trouble.
So we will not be afraid,
even if the earth is shaken
and mountains fall into the ocean depths;
even if the seas roar and rage,
and the hills are shaken by the violence. . . .

The Lord Almighty is with us;
the God of Jacob is our refuge!

Come, see what the Lord had done!
See what amazing things he has done on earth!
He stops wars all over the world;
he breaks bows, destroys spears,
and sets shields on fire!
He says,
"Stop your fighting, and know that I am God,
supreme among the nations,
supreme over the world!"

The Lord Almighty is with us;
the God of Jacob is our refuge!

Day five

During World War II, 8 men crashed in the Pacific.
Daily prayer sessions
helped them survive 21 days afloat on rubber rafts.
One of the psalms they prayed was Psalm 139.
If it helps, picture yourself as one of the survivors,
praying it on a raft with the other survivors:

Lord, you have examined me, and you know me.
You know everything I do;
from far away you understand all my thoughts.

You see me, whether I am working or resting;
you know all my actions.
Even before I speak
you already know what I will say.

You are all around me, on every side;
you protect me with your power.
Your knowledge of me is overwhelming;
it is too deep for me to understand.

Where could I go to escape from your Spirit?
Where could I get away from your presence?

If I went up to heaven, you would be there;
if I lay down in the world of the dead,
you would be there.
If I flew away beyond the east,
or lived in the farthest place in the west,
you would be there to lead me,
you would be there to help me. . . .

I praise you because you are to be feared;
all you do is strange and wonderful. . . .
God how difficult your thoughts are for me;
how many there are!

Day six

On Sunday, July 20, 1969 at exactly 3:18 p.m.,
the first manned spacecraft from Earth
came to rest on the powdery surface of the moon.

Later in the afternoon,
astronauts Armstrong and Aldrin placed on the moon
a specially prepared capsule.
It contained Psalm 8:

Lord, our Lord,
your greatness is seen in all the world. . . .

When I look at the sky,
which you have made,
at the moon and the stars,
which you have set in their places—
what is man, that you think of him;
mere man, that you care for him?

Yet you made him
inferior only to yourself;
you crowned him with glory and honor.
You made him ruler over all you have made;
you place him over all things:
sheep and cattle, and wild animals too;
the birds and the fish,
and all the creatures in the seas.

Lord, our Lord,
your greatness is seen in all the world!

Day seven

After the Last Supper,
Jesus and his disciples went to Gethsemane.
On the way they sang Psalms 115–119.
If it helps, imagine yourself present with the group
as they walk along under the stars:

The Lord is with me, I will not be afraid;
what can men do to me. . . .
The stone which the builders rejected as worthless,
turned out to be the most important of all.

This was done by the Lord;
what a wonderful sight it is!
What a wonderful day the Lord has given us;
let us be happy, let us celebrate!

While on the cross, Jesus prayed Psalm 22:

My God, my God,
why have you abandoned me?. . .
I am no longer a man; I am a worm,
despised and scorned by all. . . .
"You relied on the Lord," they say.
"Why doesn't he save you?". . .

My strength is gone,
gone like water spilled on the ground.
All my bones are out of joint;
my heart feels like melted wax inside me.
My throat is as dry as dust. . . .

All my bones can be seen.
My enemies look at me and stare;
they divide my clothes among themselves
and gamble for my robe.

5

You:
the
converser

Human relationships

"Charlie, how is your wife?"
"She's fine, I think."
"You think? Don't you know?"
"Well, she and I aren't talking."
"Have you two had a fight? Aren't you getting along?"
"Oh, no, everything is fine; we just don't talk
to each other."
"How can things be fine, if you don't even
communicate?"
"Really, everything is just perfect;
we just don't feel the need to talk to each other."

If you had overheard the above conversation,
you could not be blamed for suspecting
that either Charlie or his marriage
was on the verge of cracking up.
Persons who do not communicate with each other
cannot have much of a relationship.
As a matter of fact, when we hear someone say,
"I'm not talking to her," there is an indication
that a relationship is on the rocks.

The more closely we are related to a person,
the more deeply we communicate with him.
The distance between
"How do you do," and "I love you . . ."
indicates a whole span of human relationships.

If people were asked,
"Do you have a relationship with Jesus?"
most Christians would answer, yes.
If they were asked,
"When did you last talk with him?"
most would have difficulty answering.

Stephen Doyle
"Teach Us to Pray"

Prayer is speaking

Armand Nigro writes:
"Scripture is the living word of the living God;
it is living now because God is alive now
and he hasn't changed his mind
in what he said through the inspired writers."

The place where God speaks to us most eloquently
is in the Scriptures.
Consider Jesus' words to us at the Last Supper:

A new commandment I give you:
love one another.
As I have loved you,
so you must love one another.
If you have love for one another,
then all will know that you are my disciples.
John 13: 34–35

How might we respond to these words of Jesus?
Here's one way, suggested by Victor Hoagland
in *Prayers:*

Lord, you said this to your disciples
at the Last Supper and you say it to me now:
I must love as you love.
What a challenge you have given!
Is it possible?
I look at my way of loving
and find it embarrassingly weak and limited.
There is my constant coldness
and lack of concern for others.
How can I measure myself against you?
Yet this is what you tell me to do.
"Love one another as I have loved you. . . ."

Do you command anything impossible, Lord?
I know you do not.
Like the vine,
you communicate life to the branches.
I know you must be willing to communicate
your way of loving to me.
And this is what I ask, Lord,
that I come to love as you love.
I want to follow you and be your disciple.

Prayers: For Daily and Occasional Use

This kind of "conversation meditation" with Jesus involves 2 simple steps:

- choose a gospel passage in which Jesus is speaking;

- speak to Jesus about what he says.

Caution about words

Jesus: *In your prayers do not use
a lot of meaningless words.*
Matthew 6:7

Lepers: *Jesus! Master! Have pity on us!*
Luke 17:13

Tax Man: *God, have pity on me, a sinner!*
Luke 18:13

Youth: *Good Teacher, what must I do
to receive eternal life?*
Luke 18:18

Beggar: *Jesus! Son of David!
Have mercy on me!*
Luke 18:38

Father: *I do have faith, but not enough.
Help me!*
Mark 9:24

Jesus' caution about words
leads to another point about words and prayer.
Anthony Padovano explains it this way:

*A child
cannot say why a balloon fills him with joy;
a poet cannot find words
to match his wonder at the stars or the sea;
a musician is at a loss
to explain what Beethoven does to him;
a man in love
cannot express himself adequately. . . .*

*There are times when words say nothing
and when silence expresses everything.*
Belief in Human Life

Finally, Michael Lapierre
makes this helpful observation in "Progress in Prayer":

During childhood
recited prayer predominates . . .
words learned by heart or read from a book. . . .

From adolescence to manhood
meditative prayer develops. . . .
We also find spoken prayer during this period. . . .
It may be the outburst of an emotion
of joy, praise, gratefulness, sorrow. . . .

Finally, silent prayer
is the prayer of the mature man, whose soul
remains speechless in the presence of God,
aware of the inadequacy of whatever it may say,
simply content
to rest in this entrancing company.

Prayer is listening

God speaks to us through his word in Scripture.
Commenting on how to *listen* to God's word,
Armand Nigro says:

Pause between the phrases
so that the echo and meaning of the words
can sink into you slowly
like soft rain into thirsty soil.
You may want to keep repeating a word or phrase. . . .

Praying with Scripture this way
is an experience of listening to God.
Do not try to make applications
or search for profound meanings and implications
or conclusions or resolutions.
These usually "junk-up" our prayer.
Be content to listen simply and openly as a child.

Besides speaking to us through the words of Scripture,
God also speaks to us through the events of life.
Louis Evely writes in *Our Prayer:*

Even those who do not know God
sometimes recognize him suddenly
in the presence of a truly religious person, happening,
or event.
They are suddenly forced to say: "There is God. . . ."

God talks to us at a level in ourselves
that we ourselves cannot reach . . .
an inner dimension that we did not know we possessed
until he declared himself in it.

Four listeners

One day Jesus told the people about a sower
who went out to plant some seeds. Jesus said:

• Some seeds fell on a path.

These are like people who hear the word of God,
but ignore it. The word never takes root.

• Some seeds fell on poor soil.

These are like the people who hear God's word
and welcome it. But the word doesn't sink in.
Thus, when the first crunch comes,
the word is abandoned.

• Some seeds fell among thorns.

These are like people who welcome God's word.
But the word gets snuffed out slowly and subtly
by the day-to-day concerns of life.

• Finally, some seeds fell on good soil.

These are like people who hear God's word
and translate it into immediate action.
These people change themselves and the world they live in.

Mark 4:15–20 (paraphrased)

Now experiment

One day Jesus asked his disciples:

"Tell me, who do people say I am?"

"Some say that you are John the Baptist,"
they answered;
"others say that you are Elijah,
while others say that you are one of the prophets."

"What about you?" he asked them.
"Who do you say I am?"

Mark 8:27–29

Jesus taught the people who he was by a variety
of images.
During the next 7 days, listen to what Jesus says
to us in the Scriptures about each of these images.

Day one

Presence   Lord, help me to become more aware
of your presence within me.
Expel the darkness from my heart
that I may walk in the light of your truth.

Pause briefly, and open yourself to God's presence.
Then, listen prayerfully as Jesus speaks to you.

*I am the light of the world.
Whoever follows me
will have the light of life
and will never walk in the darkness.*

*Whoever believes in me,
believes not only in me
but also in him who sent me.*

*Whoever sees me,
also sees him who sent me.
I have come into the world as light,
that everyone who believes in me
should not remain in the darkness. . . .
I came, not to judge the world,
but to save it.*
John 8:12, 12:44-47

Conclude by speaking to Jesus, the light of the world,
about his words concerning:

light and darkness,
belief and unbelief,
salvation and judgment.

Day two

Presence   Lord, help me to become more aware
of your presence within me.
Your promise is my hope.

Pause briefly, and open yourself to God's presence.
Then, listen prayerfully as Jesus speaks to you.

> *I am the door for the sheep. . . .*
> *Whoever comes in by me*
> *will be saved;*
> *he will come in and go out,*
> *and find pasture. . . .*
>
> *I have come*
> *in order that they might have life,*
> *life in all its fullness.*
> John 10:7–10

Conclude by speaking to Jesus about his words
concerning:

> following him,
> salvation through him,
> fuller life in him.

Day three

Presence   Lord, help me to realize
the reality of your life-giving presence.
Open my mind to your truth
and my heart to your love.

Pause briefly, and open yourself to God's presence.
Then, listen prayerfully as Jesus speaks to you.

> *I am the resurrection and the life.*
> *Whoever believes in me will live,*
> *even though he dies;*
> *and whoever lives and believes in me*
> *will never die.*
>
> *Do you believe this?*
> John 11:25–26

Conclude by speaking to Jesus, the resurrection and the life, about his words concerning:

faith and life,
life and death,
death and resurrection.

Day four

Presence   Lord, help me to realize
your refreshing presence.
Create within me a hunger for your truth
and a thirst for your love.

Now, listen prayerfully as Jesus speaks to you:

> *I am the bread of life. . . .*
> *He who comes to me*
> *will never be hungry;*
> *he who believes in me*
> *will never be thirsty. . . .*
>
> *Everyone whom my Father gives me*
> *will come to me.*
> *I will never turn away anyone*
> *who comes to me,*
> *because I have come down from heaven*
> *to do the will of him who sent me,*
> *not my own will. . . .*
>
> *For what my Father wants is this:*
> *that all who see the Son*
> *and believe in him*
> *should have eternal life;*
> *and I will raise them to life*
> *on the last day.*
>
> John 6:35-40

Conclude by speaking to Jesus, the bread of life,
about his words concerning:

> himself and our food,
> his Father and us,
> faith and eternal life.

Day five

Presence   Lord, you know me
and you call me by my name.
Help me to listen for your voice.

Now, listen prayerfully as Jesus speaks to you:

I am the good shepherd.
As the Father knows me
and I know the Father, in the same way
I know my sheep and they know me.
And I am willing to die for them.

There are other sheep that belong to me
that are not in this sheepfold.
I must bring them, too;
they will listen to my voice,
and they will become one flock
with one shepherd.

The Father loves me
because I am willing to give up my life,
in order that I may receive it back again.
No one takes my life away from me.
I give it up of my own free will.
I have the right to give it,
and I have the right to take it back.
This is what my Father has commanded.
John 10:14–18

Conclude by speaking to Jesus, the good shepherd,
about the relationship between:

Jesus and his Father,
Jesus and us,
Jesus' death for us.

Day six

Lord,
you offer me life and guidance
every moment of my life.
Help me to open myself more fully
to your love and life.

Now, listen prayerfully as Jesus speaks to you:

"I am the way,
the truth,
and the life;
no one goes to the Father except by me.

"Now that you have known me, . . .
you will know my Father also;
and from now on you do know him,
and you have seen him."

Philip said to [Jesus],
"Lord, show us the Father;
that is all we need."

Jesus answered,
"For a long time I have been with you all;
yet you do not know me, Philip?
Whoever has seen me
has seen the Father."

John 14:6–9

Conclude by speaking to Jesus, the way, the truth,
and the life, about his words concerning:

me,
himself,
our Father.

Day seven

Presence   Lord, help me to realize
your saving presence.
Help me to grow in awareness
of your healing love.

Now, listen prayerfully as Jesus answers the
High Priest's question: "Are you the Messiah,
the Son of the Blessed God?"

> "I am, . . .
> and you will all see the Son of Man
> seated at the right side of the Almighty,
> and coming with the clouds of heaven!"
>
> The High Priest tore his robes
> and said,
> "We don't need any more witnesses!
> You heard his wicked words.
> What is your decision?"
>
> They all voted against him:
> he was guilty and should be put to death.
>
> Some of them began to spit on Jesus,
> and they blindfolded him and hit him.
>
> Mark 14:61-65

Conclude by speaking to Jesus the Messiah,
the Son of God, concerning:

> your sinfulness,
> his innocence,
> his suffering for *you*.

6
You: the assessor

It hits you suddenly

The turning point
in my life was the death of my father.
It was a funny thing. Here you're watching this
beautiful guy with white hair lying in his bed,
dying of a heart attack.
You hear him ramble and wander and talk about
his life:
"I was never anything. . . .
I didn't mean anything. . . ."
You watch death. Then you say, "Wait a minute.
What's going on with him is going to hit me.
What am I doing between now and my death? . . ."
You begin to assess yourself and that's a shock.
I didn't come up smelling like a rose.

Walter Lundquist
Working

Life critique

Experts in the spiritual life
recommend a regular assessment of one's daily life.
This is particularly true of spiritual directors
in the Western tradition of spirituality.
One model for evaluating your daily performance
is a technique developed by Ignatius of Loyola.
It has 5 simple steps:

Thanksgiving

Place yourself in your Father's presence.
Next, review his gifts to you during the day.
Finally, give thanks for these gifts.

Illumination

Ask the Holy Spirit to help you see yourself as you are:
a son/daughter of a loving Father,
but also needing healing.

Assessment

Using Jesus as a norm, inventory your day.
For example, what thoughts/words/actions
were most/least praiseworthy?
How might you improve tomorrow's efforts?

Forgiveness

Like the prodigal son, open your heart
to your Father's forgiveness for failures.

Conclusion

Ask the Father, Son, and Holy Spirit
to help you to do better tomorrow.

A self-critique of this kind can be made anywhere:
while walking outdoors
or kneeling in the privacy of your own room.

The best time for a self-assessment is at night.
Actually, it makes an ideal prayer.
The time should not be shorter than 5 minutes,
nor longer than 10 minutes.
For beginners, it is usually best to start with a
shorter time and to lengthen it gradually.
Equal time need not be given to each of the 5 points.

Point of focus

Nathaniel Hawthorne, the American writer,
was dead.
On his desk lay the outline of a play
that he never got a chance to write.

The play centered around a man
who never appeared on stage.
Everyone talked excitedly about him;
everyone wanted to meet him;
everyone waited for him.

All kinds of minor characters appeared on stage,
but the main character never appeared.
Eventually, the play ends.
The main character never appears.

Hawthorne's play
is a story about Everyman—about you and me,
about your life and my life.

The real you and the real me—
the main characters in our lives—rarely appear.
Instead, all kinds of minor characters do:
the sinner in me, the skeptic, the coward.
These minor players steal the show.
Meanwhile, the real you and the real me never appear.
Why?

Perhaps part of the answer lies in not knowing
how to take control of your life.
Assuming control of your life
is the idea behind the "point of focus."

This refers to the practice of centering attention
on a particular virtue you would like to build up
or a particular vice that you would like to eliminate.

For example,
you may wish to eliminate the fault of bragging.
Or you may wish to strive to become more aware
of the needs of others.
Thus, you focus special attention on this particular
fault or virtue.

Your nightly check-up might consist merely in this.
Was your performance during the day in this area:

> Excellent
> Good
> Average
> Fair
> Poor

How do you account for your successes/failures?
How might you improve tomorrow?

Some people find it helpful to keep a daily record
of successes and failures.
But this should be done only if you feel it helps
you personally.

Meditation critique

Many spiritual directors recommend
an occasional critique of one's meditation.
This means that right after your prayer period,
you take a few moments to evaluate how well it went.
If it went well, you thank God.
If not, you try to find out why.

- Did you prepare body/mind properly?

- Did you put yourself in God's presence
  and seek to remain in it?

- Did you end your prayer
  talking to God as a loving Father?

- Did anything special strike you during
  your prayer: God's presence, peace,
  an insight into God, yourself, or life?

Concerning difficulties in meditation,
Ralph Martin makes several helpful observations:

Dryness
is perhaps the most common difficulty.
Whether one week, one month, or one year
after initial conversion or renewal,
it is almost certain to come.

Dryness consists in not experiencing
the presence of God or the desire to pray.
God may seem absent or distant;
we may feel we are talking to ourselves.
It becomes difficult to persist in prayer
under such circumstances; if understood correctly,
these can be special times of grace. . . .

Sometimes our failure to experience God in a
sensible manner comes through no fault of our own,
but is a normal stage in God's purification
of our desire and intention to serve and follow Him.
When we experience His presence
in a satisfying way, our feelings may become
the motive for our love of Him.
Love will not mature or deepen
unless it reaffirms its choice of the Beloved
when the consolation of experience is not there.

Some dry times are caused by normal fluctuations
in our human nature. . . .

Our experience of God will deepen
as our fidelity through dry times remains steady.
Temptations to shorten our prayer times
during these periods,
or to drop them altogether, should be resisted.

Hungry for God

Now experiment

During the next week,
use the following "dialogues" for your meditation.

Make a brief evaluation after each meditation,
jotting down conclusions in your journal.

Also, take a few minutes each night to assess
your day.
Use the 5-point program suggested earlier.

Finally, consider a point of focus:
some virtue you might like to cultivate in your life
or some fault that you would like to eliminate.

Day one

Poet:
> If you get what you want
> in your struggle for self,
> And the world makes you king for a day,
> Just go the mirror and look at yourself,
> And see what that man has to say.
>
> For it isn't your father,
> or mother, or wife,
> Who upon you their judgment will pass.
> The fellow whose verdict
> counts most in your life,
> Is the one staring back from the glass. . . .
>
> He's the fellow to please—
> never mind all the rest!
> For he's with you right up to the end.
> And you've passed your most difficult,
> dangerous test,
> If the man in the glass is your friend.
>
> You may fool the world
> down the pathway of years.
> And get pats on the back as you pass,
> But your final reward
> will be heartache or tears,
> If you've cheated the man in the glass.

Author unknown

Apostle:
> Whoever listens to the word
> but does not put it into practice
> is like a man who looks in a mirror
> and sees himself as he is.
> He takes a good look at himself
> and then goes away,
> and at once forgets what he looks like.

James 1: 23–24

Day two

Youth: I believe that Jesus entered this world of hate,
that I might enter his world of love.

I believe that Jesus reached out to me,
that I might reach out to others.

I believe that Jesus is always with me,
even though I am not always with him.

I believe that Jesus understands me,
even though I don't understand myself.

I believe that God is my Father,
because Jesus has treated me like a brother.

Jesus: *If you have faith . . .*
you can say to this hill,
"Get up and throw yourself in the sea."
If you do not doubt in your heart,
but believe, . . .
it will be done for you.

For this reason I tell you:
When you pray and ask for something,
believe that you have received it,
and you will be given whatever you ask for.

And when you stand praying,
forgive anything you may have against anyone,
so that your Father in heaven
will forgive your sins.

Mark 11:22–25

Day three

Poet: *To every man there openeth. . . .*
A High Way and a Low,
And every man decideth
The Way his soul shall go.

John Oxenham

Youth: *Teacher, . . . what good things must I do*
to receive eternal life? . . .

Jesus: *If you want to be perfect,*
go and sell all you have
and give the money to the poor,
and you will have riches in heaven;
then come and follow me.

When the young man heard this
he went away sad,
because he was very rich.

Matthew 19:16-22

Poet: *There is a tide in the affairs of men,*
Which, taken at the flood
leads on to fortune;
Omitted, all the voyage of life
Is bound in shallows and in miseries:
And we must take the current
when it serves,
Or lose our ventures.

William Shakespeare

Day four

Knight: I call out to Him in the dark
        but no one seems to be there.

Death: *Perhaps no one is there.*
        Ingmar Bergman
        The Seventh Seal

Voice: I often wonder, God.
        Are you real,
        or are you just a wish?

        I often wonder, God.
        Do you have a face,
        or are you just a word?

        I often wonder, God.
        Do you ever speak,
        or don't I ever hear?

        I often wonder, God.
        Do I have a Father,
        or am I just an orphaned child?

Philip: *Lord, show us the Father;*
        that is all we need. . . .

Jesus: *Whoever has seen me*
        has seen the Father. . . .
        Do you not believe, Philip,
        that I am in the Father
        and the Father is in me? . . .
        Believe me that I am in the Father
        and the Father is in me.
        John 14:8–11

Day five

Prophet: *Say to those who are frightened:*
"Be strong, fear not!
Here is our God,
he comes to save us."
Isaiah 35:4

People: Lord of the sea and winds,
calm the storm when we are frightened.

Lord of the loaves and fishes,
be our food when we are hungry.

Lord of the lambs and flocks,
seek us out when we are lost.

Lord of signs and wonders,
show yourself when we have doubts.

Lord of the blind and lame,
take our hand when we grow weak.

Lord of fields and flowers,
care for us when others don't.

Lord of all that lives,
be our God; we are your people.

Jesus: *Do not be afraid . . .*
because I am with you.
Acts 18:9–10

Day six

Youth: I pray because I am a man,
and to do what a man must do,
I need strength.

I pray because there is much confusion
in my life,
and to know what is right I need light.

I pray because I have doubts,
and to keep growing in my faith
I need help.

I pray because I must make decisions,
but the choices are not always clear,
so I need guidance.

I pray because most of what I have
has been given to me,
and I ought to give thanks.

I pray because Jesus prayed to his Father,
and if he considered it important, so do I.

Jesus: *In your prayers do not use
a lot of meaningless words, as the pagans do,
who think that God will hear them
because of their long prayers.*

*Do not be like them;
your Father already knows what you need
before you ask him.
This, then, is how you should pray:
"Our Father in heaven."*

Matthew 6:7–9

Day seven

Man: I travel an unknown land
toward an unknown city.
The road is dark and misty.
Soaring mountains and roaring winds
and waters block my path.
I fear!

Jesus: *I will be with you always,*
to the end of the age.
Matthew 28:20

Man: Where are you, Jesus?
I call to you in my trouble,
but my only answer is an empty echo.

Where are you, Jesus?
I reach out to touch your hand,
but all I feel is blowing sand.

Where are you, Jesus?
I search for you in every place,
but all I find is empty space.

Jesus: *Where two or three*
come together in my name,
I am there with them.
Matthew 18:20

7
You:
the
sharer

I am there

Sharing our meditation with fellow believers
is a new experience for many people.
For many, also, it has resulted in the rediscovery
of meaningful prayer.

Whether the shared prayer consists of sharing
"peak" or "depth" experiences,
or whether it focuses on sharing prayerful insights
on Scripture, is unimportant.
The important thing is the sharing or praying together.
Jesus said:

*"Where two or three come together in my name,
I am there with them."*

Matthew 18:20

Alive

At 3:30 in the afternoon of October 12, 1972,
a chartered plane carrying a Uruguayan rugby
team crashed high up in the Andes Mountains.
Plunging into deep snow,
the plane skidded wildly and broke into pieces.
Incredibly, 28 survived the crash:

The scene was one of utmost desolation.
All around them was snow
and beyond, on three sides,
the sheer gray walls of the mountains. . . .

It was bitterly cold, and many of the boys
were in their shirt sleeves.
Some wore sports coats and others blazers.
None was dressed for subzero temperatures,
and few suitcases could be seen
which might provide extra clothes. . . .

Marcelo Perez [team captain]
directed that the wounded should be carried out
so that those who were fit
could clear the tangled seats from the floor
of the Fairchild.

As night closed in,
the 28 survivors huddled together to stay warm
in the shell of the crashed plane.

On the 8th day, search parties from Chile,
Argentina, and Uruguay abandoned their efforts
to locate the crashed plane. This news reached
the survivors over the plane's radio receiver,
which one of the boys had restored to operation.

The crash victims now realized that
they were on their own if they hoped to survive.

On the 10th day,
the survivors made an agonizing decision.
Rather than die of starvation, they decided
to eat the frozen bodies of their dead comrades.

In the torturous days that followed,
12 more survivors died (8 in a snow avalanche
that nearly killed the entire group).

Clinging tenaciously to life, the remaining 16 boys
formed themselves into an ordered society.
Tasks were assigned
according to skill and physical fitness.

Another important decision the group made
was to hold nightly prayer sessions together.

At around nine o'clock,
when the moon had disappeared over the horizon,
they would stop talking. . . .
Carlitos would start the rosary. . . .
They found great comfort . . .
in praying to the Mother of God . . .
as if she was in a better position to understand
how much they longed to return to their families.

And boys who weren't particularly religious
began to experience an unusual presence
at these nightly prayer sessions:

Even before the accident
Arturo had been a brittle, difficult person,
closed and silent even in his own family. . . .

In the plane he lay alone,
his wide green eyes staring out of his emaciated face,
a small beard on his chin. . . .

One night . . .
Arturo asked if he could lead the rosary.
They agreed that he should,
and Paez handed him his beads. . . .
He spoke with such feeling in his voice
that the other eighteen . . .
were struck with new affection for him.
When he had finished the five decades
they were all silent; only Arturo himself
could be heard weeping softly. . . .
Pedro looked at him
and asked him why he was crying.
"Because I am so close to God," Arturo replied.

Days inched slowly into weeks.
Finally in the 8th week the weather began to break.
Two of the strongest boys agreed
to try to descend the treacherous mountains.
A sleeping bag and snowshoes were made
from wreckage. Sunglasses were cut from the
dead pilot's plastic folder.

When preparations were complete,
the two boys began to descend the hostile mountains,
an almost impossible feat for even skilled
mountaineers:

It was extremely difficult going,
for while the sides of the mountain were not sheer
they were very steep
and often made up not of solid rock but of shale.
The two were attached by a long nylon luggage
strap. . . .

Their knees felt weak and wobbly,
yet both knew
that a single slip might send them both toppling
down the mountain. . . .
Canessa began a continuous dialogue with God.
He had seen the film of Fiddler on the Roof
and remembered how Tevye had spoken to God as a friend;
he now took the same tone with his Creator.
"You can make it tough, God," he prayed,
"but don't make it impossible."

On the 9th day of their torturous descent
the two boys reached the end of the mountain country:

As Parrado stood there,
his face wet with tears of joy,
Canessa came up behind him. . . .
Then both boys staggered forward off the snow
and sank onto rocks by the side of the river.
There amid birds and lizards,
they prayed aloud to God, thanking Him
with all the fervor of their youthful hearts.

The next day,
the two boys made contact with civilization.
Within hours, army helicopters were chopping
their way to the top of the mountains
to rescue the 14 remaining boys.

Summing up the group's 70-day ordeal,
one boy—chosen to speak for all—
said at a public assembly:

When one awakes in the morning
amid the silence of the mountains
and sees all around the snow-capped peaks—
it is majestic, sensational, something frightening—
one feels alone, alone,
alone in the world but for the presence of God.
For I can assure you that God is there.
We all felt it, inside ourselves,
not because we were the kind of pious youths
who are always praying all day long. . . .
Not at all. But there one feels the presence of God.
One feels, above all,
what is called the hand of God,
and allows oneself to be guided by it. Pancho Delgado

Piers Paul Read
Alive

Now experiment

Sharing meaningful experiences and prayer,
as did the boys in their nightly sessions,
can help us to grow together in love of God
and love of one another.

Here is a series of exercises
which may be used by groups to progress
from sharing meaningful experiences to sharing
personal prayer.

If circumstances make sharing with others an
impossibility, treat the matter as you would any
ordinary meditation.

Session one

Leader: Lord Jesus, we believe
that you are present with us now
as we gather in your name.

Reader: A reading from "What Man Can Be"
by Bob Richards:

*The International Olympics committee
had accepted canoe racing for the first time.
Bill Havens of Arlington, Va., was a member
of the Washington, D.C., Canoe club,
and his four-man team was going to Paris.
But as the time drew nearer,
it became clear that Bill's wife
would have her baby while he was away.
In those days there was no commercial flying
back and forth across oceans. Bill hesitated.
His wife implored him to go;
but the more he thought, the more he felt
his first responsibility was to be near her.
He withdrew.
The canoe team went to Paris without him,
and news of their win arrived
a week before Bill's son, Frank, was born.*

*Bill Havens never mentioned his disappointment
over missing out on the Olympics,
and the years passed. Then came July, 1952.
A cable arrived from Helsinki, Finland,
where the Olympics were on:
"Congratulations, Pop," the cable read,
"I won. I'm bringing home the gold medal
you lost while waiting for me to be born."
That baby, Frank, who had been responsible
for Bill's turning down the Olympics of 1924,
had won the main event in singles canoeing.*

Leader: Let us now reflect in prayerful silence,
for 4 or 5 minutes, on this question:
Did I ever make a sacrifice which,
like Bill Havens' sacrifice,
resulted in an unexpected reward?

(Silent Period)

Leader: Let us now share the fruit of our prayer
and reflection.

(Sharing Period)

Leader: Let us listen to the words of Isaiah,
the prophet, and reflect upon them
for a brief period in silence:

Reader: *My thoughts are not your thoughts,*
nor are your ways my ways,
says the Lord.

As high as the heavens are
above the earth,
so high are my ways above your ways
and my thoughts above your thoughts.
55:8–9

(Silent Period)

Leader: Father,
we have shared with each other
the love of your Son,
and the fellowship of the Holy Spirit.
May we go forth to share with others
what we have received.

Session two

Leader: Lord Jesus, we believe
that you are present with us now
as we gather in your name.
We ask that you guide everything
we do and say with your light and love.

Make yourselves comfortable—
lie on the floor, if you wish.

(Adjustment Period)

Now follow these instructions closely
and in silence:

Close your eyes and relax yourself completely.
Begin with your face muscles (pause),
shoulders (pause), arms and torso (pause),
legs and feet (pause).
If you still feel any tenseness anywhere, relax it.

Now observe your breathing.
Don't change it; just observe it (pause).

I would now like to invite you to take a fantasy trip.
Follow my instructions closely:

When you are ready, mentally—that is, in your
imagination—get up and leave this room.
Using any means of transportation you want,
go to a place of your choice. (10-second pause.)

Where are you? (pause.)
Look around; what do you see? (pause.)
Do you hear any sounds? Listen carefully. (pause.)

Are you alone, or is someone with you? (pause.)
Do you feel comfortable in this place? (pause.)
Does it make you feel happy or sad—peaceful,
secure? (pause.)

What do you feel like doing in this place? (Pause.)
Do it! (pause.)
Do you feel like saying anything? (pause.) Say it!

Why do you think you did or said what you did?
(pause.)
Why do you think you came to this place? (pause.)

Is there anything else you would like to say or do?
(pause.) Do it. (Long pause.)

For the next 4 or 5 minutes, just remain in this
place, doing what you wish.

(Silent Period)

Leader: Now, when you are ready, but only when
            you are ready, slowly return to this room.
            Don't hurry.
            When you are back, don't move;
            just open your eyes.
            I will signal you when all are back.

(Return Period)

            Beginning with the person on my left,
            share the following:
            Where did you go? Were you alone?
            What did you do?
            Did you enjoy the experience?

(Sharing Period)

Leader: Let us read the words of the apostle Paul
to the Corinthians and reflect upon them
for a brief period in silence:

Reader: *I know a certain Christian man*
who fourteen years ago was snatched up
to the highest heaven
(I do not know whether this actually happened,
or whether he had a vision—only God knows).

I repeat, I know that this man
was snatched to Paradise
(again, I do not know whether this actually
happened, or whether it was a vision—
only God knows),
and there he heard things
which cannot be put into words,
things that human lips may not speak.

2, 12:2-4

(Silent Period)

Leader: Father,
we have shared with each other
the love of your Son
and the fellowship of the Holy Spirit.
May we now go forth to share with others
what we have received.

Session three

Leader: Lord Jesus, we believe
that you are present with us now
as we gather in your name.
We ask that you guide everything
we do and say with your light and love.

Psychologist Abraham Maslow said:
"Almost all people have peak experiences.
The question might be asked in terms of
the single most joyous, happiest,
most blissful moment of your life. . . ."
How did you feel differently about yourself
at that time? What did you feel like?
What were your impulses?
How did you change if you did?

Reader: Let us listen to a high-school boy's
response to these questions:

Probably,
one of the nicest feelings I ever experienced
was just last Monday.
The day before, Sunday, about 10 of us
went up to my family's cottage on Lake Michigan.
It was a cool day,
so we all went to the beach fairly well clothed.
Toward the end of the afternoon,
we built a fire and watched the sun set.

The next day I learned that one of my friends
left some of his clothes up at the cottage.
So I took off for it, by myself.
I enjoyed the ride because of the peacefulness
and because of the beautiful autumn colors.

When I got to our cottage, I ate lunch.
I stopped by the beach where we had been.
I walked for about a mile just looking at the water
and thinking about yesterday.
I could almost hear the voices,
like spirits, whistling through the air.

I stopped where our fire had been the day before.
There I found a piece of driftwood, on which
one of the girls had carved all of our names.
The feeling of yesterday filled me, like an echo.
I picked it up and brought it home
and gave it to her to keep for all of us
as a remembrance of a beautiful Sunday.

Barry Burdiak

Leader: Let us now reflect in prayerful silence,
          for 4 or 5 minutes, on this question:
          When did I have such an experience of
          my own? Try to recapture all of the details,
          just as the high-school boy did.

          (Silent Period)

Leader: Let us now share the fruit of our prayer
          and reflection.

          (Sharing Period)

Leader: Let us listen to the words of Mark
          and reflect upon them
          for a brief period in silence.

Reader: *Jesus took Peter, James, and John*
          with him, and led them up a high mountain
          by themselves.
          As they looked on, a change came over him,
          and his clothes became shining white,
          whiter than anyone in the world could wash them.

          Then the three disciples saw Elijah
          and Moses, who were talking with Jesus.
          Peter spoke up and said to Jesus,
          "Teacher, it is a good thing that we are here.
          We will make three tents, one for you,
          one for Moses, and one for Elijah."
          He and the others were so frightened
          that he did not know what to say.

          A cloud appeared and covered them with
          its shadow, and a voice came from the cloud,
          "This is my own dear Son—listen to him!"
          9:2-7

          (Silent Period)

Leader: Father,
          we have shared with each other
          the love of your Son
          and the fellowship of the Holy Spirit.
          May we now go forth to share with others
          what we have received.

Session four

Leader: Lord Jesus, we believe
that you are present with us now
as we gather in your name.
We ask that you guide everything
we do and say with your light and love.

Reader: A reading about life:

*There comes a time in a man's life
when he must stop dreaming
about what he wishes he were.
He must accept himself as he is.*

*This does not mean
that he resigns himself to mediocrity
and stops setting goals and following ideals.
There is always room in human growth
for improvement.*

*Rather,
it means that he begins to face reality as it is.
Whatever his looks or build
he does not wish they were otherwise.*

*Similarly,
if a person does not have great intellectual ability,
he does not feel cheated.
He does not complain about it, or try to kid himself.
He accepts himself as he is.
He even reaches a point
where he rejoices in who he is.
He is happy that he is different,
and not a carbon copy of someone else.*

Leader: Let us now reflect in prayerful silence,
for 4 or 5 minutes, on this question:
What is one thing about myself, or my
life, that I found—still find—hard to accept?

(Silent Period)

Leader: Let us now share the fruit of our prayer
and reflection.

(Sharing Period)

Leader: Let us listen to the words of the apostle
Paul to the Galatians:

Reader: *If someone thinks he is something,
when he really is nothing,
he is only fooling himself.*

*Each one
should judge his own conduct for himself.
If it is good, then he can be proud
of what he himself has done,
without having to compare it
with what someone else has done.
For everyone has to carry his own load.*
6:3–5

(Silent Period)

Leader: Father,
we have shared with each other
the love of your Son
and the fellowship of the Holy Spirit.
May we now go forth to share with others
what we have received.

Session five

Leader: Lord Jesus, we believe
          that you are present with us now
          as we gather in your name.
          We ask that you guide everything
          we do and say with your light and love.

Reader: A reading about life:

If you watch the late-late movies,
you may have seen the rerun of Funny Face,
a film starring Fred Astaire.

Astaire was one of the greatest dancers
Hollywood ever produced.
In one dance sequence of the film,
he knocks a top hat off his head
and catches it a moment later on his heel.
The trick that looked so effortless in the movie
took 30 camera retakes before it worked.

We can imagine
that when Astaire picked up his hat the 29th time,
the producer was ready to scratch the routine.
But Fred Astaire wouldn't hear of it.
He wasn't made that way.
Film critics say that Astaire
was prepared to make 60 retakes, if necessary.
That's the kind of performer he was.

Leader: Let us now reflect in prayerful silence,
for 4 or 5 minutes, on this question:
What is one thing in my life:
1) that I failed to persevere in and now
regret or 2) that I nearly gave up on,
but stayed with and succeeded?

(Silent Period)

Leader: Let us now share the fruit of our prayer
and reflection.

(Sharing Period)

Leader: Let us now listen to the words of Luke:

Reader: *Jesus said: "Suppose one of you should go*
to a friend's house at midnight
and tell him, 'Friend,
let me borrow three loaves of bread.
A friend of mine who is on a trip
has just come to my house
and I don't have any food for him!'
And suppose your friend should answer
from inside, 'Don't bother me!
The door is already locked,
and my children and I are in bed. . . .'

"I tell you, even if he will not get up and
give you the bread because he is your friend,
yet he will get up and give you everything
you need because you are not ashamed
to keep on asking.
And so I say to you: Ask, and you will
receive; seek, and you will find;
knock, and the door will be opened to you."
11:5-9

(Silent Period)

Leader: Father,
we have shared with each other
the love of your Son
and the fellowship of the Holy Spirit.
May we now go forth to share with others
what we have received.

Session six

Leader: Lord Jesus, we believe
that you are present with us now
as we gather in your name.
We ask that you guide everything
we do and say with your light and love.

Now follow these instructions closely
and in silence:

Close your eyes and relax yourself completely.
Begin with your face muscles (pause),
shoulders (pause), arms and torso (pause),
legs and feet (pause).
If you still feel any tenseness anywhere, relax it.

Now I am going to read a brief passage.
Try to see, feel, hear, smell, taste everything
that is described (pause and then read reflectively):

*We had spent several weeks in southern Spain,
at the hottest time of the year.
Every morning my young son went to the balcony
of our hotel to see what kind of day it would be,
and every day it was the same—inexhaustibly sunny—
until one morning I heard a whoop of joy
and the exultant words, "Hurray! It's raining!"*

*Glorious to see the dusty streets and rooftops
running with rain!
Delightful to breathe the cleansed air,
to smell the wet earth!*

*Through the whole of that streaming day,
Longfellow's poem sang in my mind:*

"How beautiful is the rain!
After the dust and heat,
In the broad and fiery street,
In the narrow lane,
How beautiful is the rain!" (pause.)

Elizabeth Starr Hill
"Hurray! It's Raining!"

Now imagine you are lying on a deserted beach.
It has been torridly hot all day.
Suddenly a cloud appears, then a breeze,
and then drops of refreshing rain. (pause.)

See the raindrops fall on the lake,
forming millions of tiny little ringlets.
(20-second pause.)
Listen to the rain falling on the lake, the beach,
and on metal objects on or near the beach.
(20-second pause.)
Feel the rain fall on your body, soothing it,
running down your shoulders, arms, and face.
(20-second pause.)
Taste the rain as it falls on your parched lips
and trickles across them. (20-second pause.)
Smell the freshness of the air. (20-second pause.)

Now, for the next 4 or 5 minutes, just lie there,
enjoying the rain with all of your 5 senses.

(Silent Period)

Leader: Let us now open our eyes.
            Beginning with the person on my left,
            share the following:
            Did you enjoy the experience?
            What sense predominated in the experience?
            Did any special thoughts come to you?

            (Sharing Period)

Leader: Let us now listen to the words of Matthew:

Reader: *Jesus said:*
            "Look at the birds flying around:
            they do not plant seeds,
            gather a harvest, and put it in barns;
            your Father in heaven takes care of them!
            Aren't you worth much more than birds?
            Which one of you can live a few more years
            by worrying about it?. . .

            "Look how the wild flowers grow:
            they do not work
            or make clothes for themselves. . . .
            It is God who clothes the wild grass—
            grass that is here today, gone tomorrow,
            burned up in the oven. . . .

            "Your Father in heaven knows
            that you need all these things.
            Instead, be concerned
            above everything else with his Kingdom
            and with what he requires,
            and he will provide you
            with all these other things."
            6:26–33

(Silent Period)

Leader: Father,
we have shared with each other
the love of your Son
and the fellowship of the Holy Spirit.
May we now go forth to share with others
what we have received.

Session seven

Leader: Lord Jesus, we believe
that you are present with us now
as we gather in your name.
We ask that you guide everything
we do and say with your light and love.

Reader: A reading from *Nobel* by Nicholas Halasz:

One morning . . .
Nobel awoke to read his own obituary.
The obituary was printed
as a result of a simple journalistic error . . .
Any man would be disturbed
under the circumstances, but to Alfred Nobel
the shock was overwhelming.
He saw himself as the world saw him—
"the dynamite king," the great industrialist . . .
None of his true intentions—the breakdown
of barriers that separated men and ideas—
was recognized or given consideration.
As he read his obituary with horror,
Nobel resolved to make clear to the world
the true meaning and purpose of his life.
[This could be done through the final disposition
of his fortune.] His last will and testament
would be the expression of his life's ideals. . . .
The result was the most valued of prizes
given to those who had done the most
for the cause of world peace.

Leader: Let us now reflect in prayerful silence,
for 4 or 5 minutes, on this question:
If you were asked to write your own obituary
for tomorrow morning's paper,
what would you list as the achievement
you are most proud of in your life—and why?

(Silent Period)

Leader: Let us now share the fruit of our prayer
         and reflection.

(Sharing Period)

Leader: Let us now listen to the words of Luke:

Reader: *Jesus said:*
         "A rich man had land which bore good crops.
         He began to think to himself,
         "I don't have a place to keep all my crops.
         What can I do?

         "'This is what I will do,' he told himself;
         'I will tear my barns down
         and build bigger ones,
         where I will store the grain'. . . .

         "But God said to him, 'You fool!
         This very night
         you will have to give up your life;
         then who will get all these things
         you have kept for yourself?'"
         12:16–20

(Silent Period)

Leader: Father,
         we have shared with each other
         the love of your Son
         and the fellowship of the Holy Spirit.
         May we now go forth to share with others
         what we have received.

Appendix

Spiritual direction program

Three years ago,
the author sent a letter to a number of students
in the high school in which he teaches.
The letter read:

Dear _____,

A number of students and faculty members
would like to see St. Ignatius strive not only for
academic leadership, but also spiritual leadership.
From my observations of you, I feel that you might
be open to a proposal I would like to make to you,
personally. I put it in writing because I don't
want you to feel pressured in any way.

I would like to invite you to commit yourself
to 3 things:

- attendance at the Eucharistic Liturgy once
  a week (in addition to Sunday) on any school
  day of your choice;

- agreement to give 10 minutes of each day to
  meditation;

- agreement to meet with a spiritual director
  every week (or 2 weeks) for 15 minutes or so.

What is meditation? What is a spiritual director?
What do you do when you meet with him?
These are questions that cannot be answered in
words. They must be experienced.
They will unfold in the process of doing them.

If, after giving serious thought to this invitation,
you feel you would be willing to give it a try
for a few weeks or months, contact me (or one of
the other 8 directors, listed in the left-hand column).
Just give the director this letter and ask him/her
if he/she would be available to serve as your director.
Your director will take it from there.

My personal prayers for your continued spiritual
growth.

Sincerely in Christ,

The response to the letters exceeded expectation.
The directors (lay and religious) met together
in the early stages of the program for support
and to share insights.
They saw their director's role as taking a threefold
thrust:

- helping students to place a new priority
  on a spiritual life,
  and supporting them in carrying it out;

- providing students with "input" on the spiritual
  life in general, and prayer in particular;

- sharing with students their prayer experience.

This book developed out of the second point.
Each chapter of the book follows an identical format:
an "input" section and an "experiment" section.
The "input" section contains instructions on prayer
and the spiritual life.
The experiment section contains "prayer guides"
for daily meditation.

The author and his colleagues believe firmly
that every high school and youth/adult study group
contains a number of students/adults who are ready
for such a program.

The mechanics for launching the program are simple:

- Send a letter of invitation to students/adults
  you believe to be spiritually capable of such
  a program.

- Arrange a personal conference with each
  person who responds favorably.
  The author's own initial conferences followed
  these lines:
  Why did you say "yes" to this invitation?
  Ideally, what would you like to achieve at the
  end of the year as a result of this program?
  What role would you like to see me play in
  helping you to achieve your goal?
  What is the status of your "spiritual life"?
  Do you pray regularly/sometimes/rarely?
  Where, when, and how do you usually pray?
  Do you have a place at home
  where you can pray without interruption?
  If not, where do you plan to make the daily
  meditations to which you are committing
  yourself?

- The director then gives a copy of this book
  to the student/adult.
  He instructs him/her to read over the input
  section of Chapter One, underlining points
  he/she might want to discuss in next week's
  meeting. (Decide on a regular day and a
  regular time for the next eight meetings.)

- At the second meeting, the director and the
  directee discuss and clarify the input matter.
  If everything is clear, the directee begins
  his/her first week of daily meditation, following
  the prayer guides in the experiment section
  at the end of Chapter One.
  The directee also prepares the input section
  of Chapter Two for the next meeting.
  (The remaining meetings follow a similar
  format.)

An ideal follow-up meditation book to *You* is
The Mustard Seed by Mark Link, S.J.
It, too, is available from Argus Communications.